Heavenly Text

Finding Christ Within

Vol. I

Heavenly Text
Finding Christ Within

Vol. I

By
Nancy Mertzlufft

Edited by
Mary Mueller, J.D.
Sharon Troth, PhD.

Cover designed by Jenny McGee
Angel painting by Nancy Mertzlufft

Printed in the United States of America

Heavenly Text,
Finding Christ Within
Vol. I

Nancy Mertzlufft

All bible citations and quotes are from *The Jerusalem Bible,* Doubleday. 1966

ISBN 1456353349
First Printing 2010

Acknowledgements

Thanks from the depth of my heart to all those who have touched my life –- those on earth and those in heaven. You are all angels to me. All my writings are dedicated to you. You know who you are. I love you.

Judy & Bill,
many blessings —
and much peace
Nancy

Contents

Introduction

The Gifts All Are Entitled To

Introduction

God sought me. Since 1983, my life has witnessed and been filled with ultimate sorrow and ultimate joy. I had to learn that the chaos of this world and my life were but a gift to enable me to grow.

In 1983, when my daughter Pam (21), died from leukemia my faith awareness increased. I wrote a book, *Gift of Life, (1985),* about her profound acceptance of her illness and her death. After her death a newness, a flow of synchronicity, seemed to have entered my whole life, or perhaps it has always been there, and I was at last learning how to follow. I've previously had an intuitive feel, an awareness of an inner voice, that I knew was speaking to me, an inner connection, a deep knowing, a thought demanding to be recognized - a calling. Now I know this is being touched by the hand of God. I believe we all receive these "messages" in varying degrees according to our openness and willingness to receive. We just have to become aware of God's "presence" in our lives. My life has been on a high since I have adopted a mode of acceptance that something beyond me totally governs my actions. When one learns to turn from self-centered to God-centered the world's doors open.

For me, growing in my spirituality has included the whole of all religions, and of all faiths. I believe when all systems of religion are purified of human intervention and dogma, they will be identical, and all will merge back together. It appears to me that it is easier for the many individuals to engage in certain ritual patterns and religions, than to confront God directly. Personal growth and responsibility is our job here on earth. We should always be reaching for higher levels. As our minds and consciousness expand we gradually become who we are meant to be.

I feel Christ's church has been hindered down through the centuries by its almost fanatic zeal to make Christians of all people and not all people followers of Christ. Theological doctrine has been emphasized more than love and understanding. Christ belongs to all of humanity, not to religions of the world. Christ came to show us and teach us the way to salvation. He taught us that death and suffering are part of life and can be overcome. I feel Christianity has overly emphasized the suffering and crucifixion of Jesus instead of examples of how He lived His life. More attention needs to be given to Christ's Lessons of Love, His way of life, His Healings, His Resurrection, and His Ascension, which all brought about His Transfiguration.

In 1990 I felt God's nudge, His gentle push, and embarked upon writing about my faith, my quest for its meaning and my reasons for life. I'm convinced that listening to "God Messages" can become the key to peace: the peace that comes with faith - a peace that is a gift from God. Out of my gratitude to Him I have written about these gifts, the gifts I'm sure we "all" possess.

God heightened my faith awareness by profoundly involving me in a spiritual realm that demanded deep faith for its acceptance. Over a period of years, (1993-1994) I visited several apparition sites (alleged sites visited by Jesus' mother) and was blessed with seeing the spirit of Mary, His mother. Once I knew the Spirit world was real my whole outlook on life changed. Gifts resulted through supernatural occurrences. God began to communicate with me through dreams and visions. I responded to God's call. I reached the wisdom of the realm of the Spirit and knew my life would always continue in the love of God and my neighbor for the peace of my soul. I learned to become an open vessel for the power of God to manifest itself through me. Laying-on-of-hands and other healing modalities became a part of my life.

My writings center on my messages, so in essence, this book is an effort to reintroduce to others' consciousness the messages of God, Jesus, and Mother Mary. Throughout my writings I will make a small cross + that signals I am hearing a message. I will type this ("+") in order not to have to repeat my favorite, "Must be a God Message." I hope that you are in tune to your phone line to God. If not, I pray my story will enhance your ability to be aware of your God messages and you will become more eager to respond to them. The rewards are unbelievable. I have learned and know that life should be nothing more than messages from the heart.

I feel it is important to leave my writings in chronological order to demonstrate how one grows with time. To read an overview of all my writings you can visit my web site at www. nancymertzlufft.com.

The Gift of God Messages

September 30, 1982. "Pam, there's a name for what you've got. It's called acute myelocytic leukemia."

Devastating words for a parent to hear a doctor tell her daughter. I was stunned. I just stood there, holding Pam's hand, as tears rolled slowly down our cheeks. What an unexpected shock.

That day was the beginning of a very difficult time in my life. As I look back now it was the day God began opening me to His ways on a deeper level.

Pam had just turned twenty-one but she wanted her father, Erv, and I to be involved in all the discussions and decisions. We felt she was an adult and decided we would honor whatever medical/non-medical treatment she chose.

The doctor explained that her body was full of cancer and she had only a 10% chance of a cure. He was hoping for a remission. In remission the cancer is under control but it could return at any time. Pam agreed with the doctor to start a month hospital stay with a constant 24-hour chemotherapy treatment.

Immediately, the next day, she became deathly ill from the chemo. It was very evident this month was not going to be easy on any of us. Erv and I took turns at the hospital being with her around the clock. By the third day, because of pneumonia, she had to have emergency surgery on her lung.

The morning of surgery, Erv and I spent a very meaningful and memorable time with a very, very, weak Pam. We stood on either side of her bed, and she began speaking to us ever so softly.

1

Heavenly Text

"Mom, Dad, Jesus talked to me last night. He told me that this was all for a purpose. Not just for me, not just for our family, but also for many people. That he needed me to help do His work. If He can suffer and die on the cross then certainly I can do this." +

She elaborated a while longer and then suddenly said in a more pronounced way, "That sure didn't sound like me."

I commented, "No, Pam it didn't sound like you. I feel God is communicating through you to us. This is His way of letting us know it is all in His hands, and He is here with us."

I cannot describe to you the intense feeling of God's presence that we all felt. The room felt different. For me it was a hushed quiet, a warmth, a powerful mystical experience. It was a moment I felt God put His arms around me. + It was as if a shield moved around me giving me strength, Pam strength, Erv strength, all of us strength to get through what we were going to have to endure. Pam went on to expound on her love for us. She was full of praise and compliments, sharing her all as if it were her last moments with us. She told us she thought that she might die in surgery.

She survived the surgery only to have to undergo another surgery a few days later. She became weaker and weaker and I began to literally see my daughter disintegrate before my eyes.

We shared many weary days. I could go on forever with the many trials, sufferings, and unexpected happenings, but at this time I will only touch upon the profound spiritual ones. Pam's personal relationship with God became more and more evident.

One day in particular I recall an extremely moving emotional time. During one of her bone marrows the needle got stuck in her hipbone. The doctor tugged and tugged trying to get it to move to no avail. Pam was very tense. The doctor was apologizing to Pam while a nurse and I held her hands. It was evident she was in intense pain.

I leaned over and whispered in Pam's ear, "Honey, say a prayer. You'll make it."

We all heard her plead, "God, be with me. Help me. I

2

really need you."

At that moment we witnessed a miracle. I again immediately felt God's presence. + Pam relaxed her grip on our hands. The nurse looked at me in bewilderment. We both saw and felt Pam totally relax. The doctor worked for over twenty minutes trying to take the needle out.

When he was finished he profusely apologized to Pam and she replied, "Thank you, doctor, that was the easiest bone marrow we've had yet."

The three of us were astounded. The nurse commented, "The man upstairs was here. I felt it." We all agreed.

It was moments like this that got me through the ordeal of lengthy days and nights. It was a long and tiring month with many ups and downs but the unbelievable did happen. On October 26, the Doctor walked in and handed Pam a card. It was a Snoopy card. He handed it to her and she read it out loud. "You're tougher than you think gal. You have a remission."

One can only imagine the tears, hugs, and enthusiasm that filled her room. I knew in my heart that the celebration might be short lived, but she was joyous after a grueling month of tests, chemo, surgeries, and suffering.

With enthusiasm Pam said, "Mom, God has given me some extra time and we're really going to enjoy it."

She had no hair, was very feeble, and was terribly thin, (less than a hundred pounds) but she was going home. She was elated. We all were. The elation only lasted a few short weeks. When we returned to the doctor's office for a check up her blood tests revealed that the cancer had returned. The doctor explained he would have to resume chemo.

On our trip home from the doctor's office Pam said to me, "Mom, I hope you don't think I'm a chicken, but I can't go through again all I recently went through. I'm feeling better now and I just want to stay home and live until I die."

We respected her decision. And live she did. She wanted to spend quality time with her sister, Deanna (16 years of age), her brother, Joe (21 years of age), and of course her boyfriend,

Tom. Her visits with them in the hospital had been few and far between. She wanted to go see all my extended family of eight brothers and sisters in Kentucky, and Erv's extended family of eight brothers and sisters in St. Louis.

We made a trip to Kentucky and St. Louis where she gave each a gift of a personal Christmas ornament. We had spent many enjoyable emotional times buying them. She said her individual good-byes. All were deeply touched by her courage and spiritual strength.

Two months of joy filled our home with visitors, friends, and relatives. Pam made it a point to say her private good-byes to all she knew. She impressed her doctors, nurses, everyone with her positive attitude and acceptance of the inevitable. We laughed a lot, cried a lot, and overall simply lived our lives to the fullest every day.

One day her face became partially paralyzed and the doctor informed her the cancer was in her brain that it would only get worse, and she was probably going to go blind and lose her speech. She promptly announced, "God will not let that happen. I don't mind dying but I want to see and talk to my family until I do."

Since her illness it had become our habit to gather around her bed each night for prayers. With the new face problem she asked me to lay my hands on her face. She prayed fervently, we all prayed fervently, and one night after prayers she announced. "Mom, I think it worked. Your hands felt hot and I felt a tingling in my face." I agreed I felt something strange. + The next morning when she woke up her face was back to normal and remained so until the day she died.

Christmas Eve was extra special, one that we all will forever hold dear in our hearts because it was full of true love and giving. Shopping had been a joyous pleasure we had shared on her good days and she beamed as she presented each of us with her final gifts.

Christmas morning we had Mass at our home and spent a quiet day. The next day she began to go down hill rapidly. She died, at home, in the early morning hours, on January 5,

1983. I was by her side administering to her needs when I heard her whisper ever so softly, "It's Christ Light." I watched her intently as I leaned closer to her lips. Suddenly she very clearly said, "I'm so happy, I'm glad, not sad." I sighed and thanked God. She breathed lightly and said, "I'm going now." Her breathing grew shallower and then I knew she was gone. Her death was as she wanted, peaceful, and in her own bed.

It was over at last. Our Pam was free.

***

I gave my daughter back to God, and He has given me abundance in her place.

I thought I knew sorrow, but in giving up my daughter, I learned the great depth of grief. What I lived through is perhaps the most difficult of all experiences. I watched someone I loved falling from life and felt totally helpless. It was hard, and it was painful, but I came through with a greater capacity for love.

Death taught me more than I ever dreamed possible. Pam not only taught me how to die but how to live. Pam had lived her life to the fullest and she died with the same zest. We lived her death instead of running from it. I am eternally grateful to have had my daughter for twenty-one years and to share her special relationship with God.

Because of her I began to grow in my faith. I began to view life, my purpose in it in a different way. I guess one might say that I began getting my priorities in order. God became foremost in my mind. My faith awareness increased and my attempts to understand the "Whys of Life" took on new meaning. My search for all kinds of medical and spiritual knowledge increased. I wanted to understand why Pam had gotten so ill. I had a fervent longing to understand life in its entirety. No matter where I was in thought, God saw to it and continued to send the right individuals or the right books, almost mysteriously, to spur me on.

I also became more perceptive. There seemed to be a

feeling of not being alone. New thoughts demanded to be recognized. My intuition increased and began to be the divine force in my life. It was at this time I began calling intuitive nudges my "God Messages." A sense of flow of life gradually seemed to enter my whole person or perhaps it had always been there and I was at last learning how to follow. I didn't realize it at the time but my intuition was aligning me with my soul. In time I learned that this inner calling, intuition, divine guidance, was dipping into the pool of Divine Knowledge. I was gradually learning how to hear God's quiet voice in my heart. It was to be a lengthy process but I was open and willing. I was learning that the road to the soul is through the heart.

Repeatedly during her illness Pam had asked me to write a book to tell her story. I was too involved, too consumed with her and spending the last days with her, to even try to start then. I wrote many notes shortly after she died but nothing more. I really wanted to honor her wish but I didn't know where to begin. I wasn't sure I could handle the task. I spent many months going through her personal belongings and getting life back to normal. I continued to think and talk about writing but never made the real commitment until we were on vacation in the fall of 1983.

We went to Columbia, South Carolina, to visit Jim and Carolyn, longtime friends we had met through Erv's business. On Sunday morning, Erv and I went to Mass at Our Lady of the Hills Catholic Church. As I knelt down and viewed a wall hanging over the altar I began to feel the presence. + The picture was the figure of Jesus with his hands stretched out and many individuals climbing upward toward Him. There really isn't a correct way to describe what happened but I suddenly instinctively knew I had to begin to write Pam's story. The feeling was powerful. + I was overcome with emotion and began to cry. Then God confirmed. It was the first of many times that God would affirm His messages to me through sermons from a priest. This sermon was on learning to follow through with your gut feelings and intuition.

Heavenly Text

As I left church I approached the priest and thanked him for helping me make a big decision. When I got back to Carolyn's I announced that I was going to start writing the book telling Pam's story. How or what format I wasn't sure. Then all of a sudden I had an idea for an outline. + I asked for a piece of paper, and wrote down the outline that I used throughout my writings.

When I got home I began in earnest. My computer-genius son Joe (An Apple Macintosh Dealer) talked me into buying a computer. If it weren't for him and his patience, writing books would not be a way of life for me. I am a slow computer learner. He has been my savior in teaching, coaching, and solving computer problems over the years.

I'd had no previous training in writing so I just began by talking to my computer. I set a goal to write ten pages a week. If I didn't write during the week, I would write all day on Fridays. Once in a while I got industrious and did twenty or more pages a week and then I'd rest the next week. I interviewed Pam's doctors. I sent letters to all family members asking for input on how her death had affected them. In about six months' time I had finished my first manuscript.

I knew the head of the English department at the University of Missouri, Bob Barth. I asked him if he would read my manuscript. I knew he would be honest. When he called and said he thought it was publishable, I was elated. He also made some suggestions. A newspaper friend read it and gave me encouragement, "Nancy, I think you have something. Go for it." By now I could hardly contain my new enthusiasm.

A good and dear friend Shirley, who was a former English teacher offered to edit my writings for me. Then I started reading how to publish, how to submit, how to present. I was determined this was going to be published, and I knew in my heart that God wanted it to be. He had helped me write it. I sent my manuscript to about a dozen publishers. Rejections began coming in.

Then one day I got a call from New York. It was the National Catholic Reporter. They were interested in my

7

manuscript. (This was it!) I couldn't believe what I was hearing a-phone-call and I hadn't even sent them a manuscript. + Needless to say it took but about two seconds to register that I was going to be a true, honest-to-goodness, author.

I asked how they had received my manuscript. They informed me a man who had just come to work for them had received my manuscript from a friend of his in Missouri. I later found out the friend was a friend of someone I had given my text to read. Coincidence? I think not. I believe I had a special agent. He lives upstairs. + I was ecstatic.

In spring of 1984 an inexplainable intervention happened. I know without a doubt I was saved from a car wreck. +

I was on my way to deliver food to friends because of a death in their family. As I pulled out onto a narrow road that led to their home my attention went to a sign that I'd never noticed before. The sign explained a new development. I was reading it instead of paying attention to the road. All of a sudden a force other than myself made my steering wheel turn abruptly. Abruptly and with such force it hurt my wrist. I know I did not turn it. It turned on its own accord. It turned before I looked up. I then looked up and immediately in front of me a large dump truck was coming over a hill on my side of the road. If the wheels had not been turned I definitely would have been hit. I uttered a thank you to my guardian angel, because I knew without a doubt some force made my car wheels turn other than myself. My wrist hurt for several weeks. Each time my wrist gave me trouble I again thanked God, because I would remember the terror of seeing that truck. This was about the time I began to realize +'s were becoming a part of my life. I wondered if Pam was protecting me from above.

Then an accident happened with my daughter Deanna that added to the breaking of my heart. Deanna and several of her friends had been attending evening classes for several weeks to become licensed Red Cross swimming instructors. Late one night in June of 1984, after we were asleep, the phone rang. A terrified young voice belonging to Patti, a friend of Deanna's, was breathlessly telling me Deanna had been run over by a car. Patti continued, "The ambulance is on the way." I asked where she was run over and Patti started naming the location. I stated firmly "Patti, where on her body was she run over?" She hysterically exclaimed, "It's her foot. It's her foot and it looks terrible." I told Patti that Erv and I were on the way; we'd be there in five minutes, and to not let the ambulance leave before we got there. At least I knew it wasn't Deanna's head and that she'd probably be all right.

We got to the scene in time for me to ride with her in the ambulance the twenty-five miles to the hospital. Deanna tried to explain to me how a heated discussion over a boy had begun at the filling station with another girl. The girl lost her temper and had left suddenly in her car. As she sped away Deanna's foot had got caught under the car's tire. All I could think of was, "Teenagers, boys, cars," and, "Why, God?"

I remember arriving at the hospital and watching as the doctor set her foot without anesthesia. When the doctor entered the emergency room and saw the problem he immediately said, "Deanna, I'm sorry but I have to set this right now." It only took a fraction of a minute but I knew the pain from Deanna's grip. She nearly squeezed my hand off. The doctor then explained that her foot was only hanging by ligaments and that if he didn't act quickly, she would loose her foot because there was no blood flow from the ankle to the foot.

Immediate surgery, three hours, five screws, and two pins later she began her seven day stay in the hospital. The doctors were not sure she would walk correctly again. I remember sitting in that hospital room around the clock and not believing I was there again. But Deanna was alive. I was grateful.

Months later they removed the hardware and she began physical therapy. She went to school on crutches the majority of her senior year but with lots of exercise and plenty of determination, she began to walk properly again. Not even a limp. ("Thanks, God".)

In the summer of 1985 we had a joyous occasion. The completed published book, *Gift of Life*, arrived at my home. The feelings of joy and accomplishment overwhelmed me. I felt so proud knowing Pam's life of learning how to die was going to be helping many. That night I received a huge + I'll explain. It's the story of Tiger.

***

Back in 1979 we had a stray, wild cat arrive at our home. Sissy, our Collie, accepted her and she became a good pet, which we named "Cat." Cat eventually had a litter of kittens; but Cat died when they were only one day old. The kids and I were disappointed and I decided to come to the kittens' rescue. I bought a baby doll bottle and began feeding them several times each day. Only one of the four kittens lived and we named him "Tiger." He was so tiny that I would hold him in the palm of my hand to feed him. As he got older Sissy let him nurse with her litter of pups.

Obviously, Tiger thought he was a person, maybe a dog, but he lived and remained in our family for many years. He was totally an outside cat, but when he would see me, he would always jump from the ground, up into my arms. Tiger and I had developed a special bonding with all those feedings.

In the fall of 1982, when Pam was ill, Joe and Deanna decided to ride their bikes into town, which is about four miles from our home. Before they left Joe put needed air in the tire of his bike. When they got in town they called requesting someone to come in with the air pump because the tire had again gone flat. Erv went in to meet them. When Erv opened the trunk of the car out jumped Tiger. They all laughed and presumed Tiger had jumped in the trunk when they had used the pump the first time. Joe says it was like, "Hi, guys, I came too. " Then all of a sudden a stray dog came running across the parking lot. A terrified Tiger took off. Joe and Deanna ran after him, but to no avail. They called and called but could never find him.

I went to the area several hours later and walked the streets calling his name with no luck. We ran an ad in the newspaper. No responses. We finally decided Tiger had found a home where they would let him live inside. He had chosen that home over ours. Tiger had always wanted to live inside, but several in our family were allergic to cats, and the garage was as far as he got on cold nights. We missed him and never gave up the hope that he might return.

While Pam was ill she often wondered if she would be able to communicate with us after her death. She enjoyed thinking up all kinds of ways she would keep in touch. One day she said, "I know, when I'm on the other side I'll bring Tiger home."

In the evening of the day that *Gift of Life* arrived, Erv and I were sitting on the screened-in-porch reminiscing about Pam, when suddenly I thought I heard a cat, (in the dark) out back. I opened up the back door to investigate and a cat jumped into my arms. I couldn't believe it. Shocked, I shouted, it's "Tiger." + (He'd been missing for nearly three years.) Erv insisted it wasn't Tiger until I pointed out the cat's ear. Tiger had been in a fight one day and had lost half of one ear. This cat in my arms only had a half of one ear. I sat on the porch, holding him, crying with joy, reliving Pam's words (I'll bring him home). I felt that presence again. I fed Tiger and loved him to pieces. To me, it was a special thank you from Pam and God, congratulating me on my book. I put Tiger in the garage that night. The next day he disappeared. We never saw him again.

***

Some people just travel the road of life straight down the middle, avoiding any rough spots. Others, by accident or design, manage to hit every pothole and patch of loose gravel. The latter fits our family. My belief in miracles took on a new dimension when dealing with yet more tragedies in my life. It's hard to believe, but in the next year our daughter Deanna was involved in two more accidents. She survived, wiser, more mature, and appreciates life more. I became much more aware of my intuition, my heart, my "God Messages." How else could I have gotten through it all? I'll explain.

On Good Friday, April 1986, around five in the evening, a hysterical voice was screaming into the phone, "Mrs. Mertzlufft, Deanna has been in a wreck, they are taking her to the hospital in a helicopter. I thought you would want to know."

Deanna had picked up a friend from college to come spend Easter with us. On their ride home, as they discussed their first college months, Deanna had hit a patch of rocks on the side of the road, which made her lose control of her car. Her car went into a spin and was hit by an oncoming vehicle. She was thrown out the rear window of her car and her friend flew out the side door.

When we arrived at the emergency room the doctor told us he suspected a broken neck, hemorrhaging in the brain, and a collapsed lung. Visually we could see massive facial injuries, which would require plastic surgery. I could have put my fist through the wound on her forehead that extended from her eyebrows into her hairline.

Scans and tests began and the prognosis improved as the night went on. Her neck was not broken. There was massive strain and ligament damage to the neck but the head injury was external, no brain damage.

Her friend did not fare as well. She died that evening from her injuries. It was a very difficult time. It was very painful to see Deanna suffer through being the driver of a car in which her friend was killed. Our hearts ached for the other family. We understood the tremendous grief of losing a child. We naturally felt somewhat responsible, as most parents do when their children are involved. We were all devastated. Deanna's extreme sorrow became my sorrow.

Deanna struggled through another long recovery period, but she was alive. After a hospital stay of about two weeks, she started looking and feeling better emotionally and physically. I continued to worry about her emotional state. The ordeal had created another scar in my heart.

A few months later, in October of 1986, another phone call came around midnight. I was startled awake and said to Erv. "You don't suppose it's Deanna... "Erv said, "No, Nancy you worry too much." Within seconds I could tell by his responses that there was another problem. He was talking to a nurse in an emergency room.

This time it was a hit and run accident. A car hit both Deanna and her date as they walked across a street at an intersection in downtown Columbia. The car was going fifty miles an hour in a twenty mile per hour zone. Deanna was very seriously injured. Her pelvis was broken in several places, her bladder was ruptured, her shoulder was separated and broken in three places, all of the ligaments were blown out of her left knee, and she was a mass of bruises. Her male friend had a skull fracture and a knee injury.

This time it was a hospital stay of three weeks. We were beginning to feel like permanent fixtures at the hospital. Because she had blown all the ligaments out of her knee the doctor cast her leg in hopes that scar tissue would grow. He would then be able to possibly have something to tie to in later surgery. He said her cast needed to be on for at least two months.

Deanna and I began a daily ritual. I would lay my hands on her cast and pray for a healing, "Please, God, no more surgery." When the cast came off the doctor was shocked how she had improved and only sent her to physical therapy for an extended time. Surgery was not required. + Fearing no one would believe me I did not talk about the possibility of a healing. I did not doubt that God could have used me, if He so desired.

For two years, this child had been a constant worry. I

wondered if she was ever going to grow up. You can't imagine the constant fear I lived in. I jumped every time the phone rang. I couldn't believe all of this could happen to one person. I knew I was learning compassion, patience, and perseverance, because when it happened to her, it happened to me. The fact that she walks today with absolutely no limp, looks radiant, with no visible facial scars, and is able to carry on her life is a miracle.

Amidst all the problems over the past years we also had enjoyable and wonderful memories. On November 2, 1985, our son Joe married a lovely girl named Kathy. Kathy is from St. Louis and they met while she was attending the University here in Columbia. We were happy to see our family begin to grow. Deanna was even able to be in the wedding between accidents.

Then in 1988 Deanna got married in late August to Jeff, a young man she had met while attending a business school in St. Louis.

With Deanna and Joe married and gone our large home in the country was no longer needed. We put it up for sale. It sold immediately.

We bought a home to renovate while we built our dream home. Erv and I were both personally very involved in the renovation of the temporary residence and actual building of our new home. We moved into our new home in August of 1989. In nine months' time we had had a wedding, moved, refurbished and redecorated a house and built a new home. To say the least, it had been a whirlwind of a year.

Then it was my turn for physical problems. My left foot had been giving me trouble for some time and it finally reached a point that I could hardly walk. I'd worn it out. I went to a doctor who said I needed surgery, but he refused to operate because of the massive amount of problems. He said I needed a foot specialist. The closest one we could find was in Tulsa, Oklahoma. This doctor thought my problem was a Neuron in my foot and he decided to operate by making an incision in the top of my foot. This was September of 1990. After several months I wasn't any better. The doctor decided he had not gotten the entire nerve and operated again on my foot in January of 1991.

After the second surgery, I still felt no better and was very, very, discouraged. I was trying prescription inserts in my shoes, therapy, you name it, but nothing was working. I was feeling depressed, alone, helpless, and didn't know what to do next. Crutches and walkers weren't my idea of fun. I kept calling on God to please help me to understand, "Why was all of this happening?"

Then one night I had a very pronounced dream in which I saw the inside of my foot. + It was like looking at an X-Ray. I could see a configuration of darkness in my foot. I knew the problem was still there. I could see it. But I didn't know where to turn with my new information and thought probably no one would believe me.

In time, I fortunately heard of a foot doctor who was new to the St. Louis area. I made an appointment. He wanted to cut open the bottom of my foot and investigate. This scared me to death. I didn't agree. Instead I decided to go to the Mayo Clinic in Minnesota to get another opinion. They also wanted to go in through the bottom of my foot to try to solve the problem. I was distraught.

It was an extremely hard decision. Since my quality of life was almost non-existent I decided to have another surgery. The doctors advised waiting a few months so that the previous surgeries could better heal. I decided I'd use the doctor in St. Louis for the surgery since it would be closer for follow-up visits.

August 13, 1991. I had a profound and powerful dream. In my dream, I realized a tree was having trouble and I said, "I can help." I remember vomiting. Then little birds came, picked up the vomit, and placed it on the branches of this massive tree. Each time the birds placed the vomit, a beautiful flowering bud popped out. I woke up saying, "prolificate, prolificate, prolificate."

The word kept repeating itself in my mind all day. When I looked up "prolific" in the dictionary it said, highly fruitful, abundant, or highly productive, such as a "prolific writer".

I decided the dream must be a + telling me to begin to write again. I started keeping a journal.

Then in January 1992, I had the third foot surgery. The operation, making an incision in the bottom of my foot, went smoothly. The first thirty-six hours were rough, but after that I just needed plenty of down time to let it heal. When I went back for my check-up the doctor said he had found a very unusual mass in my foot. He explained that all of the nerves in that area of my foot had somehow meshed together into one clump. He said that he had never seen anything like it. He decided I must have been born with the problem, and that my foot had finally just given out. He felt the other surgeries had only aggravated the situation. He drew me a picture to visually explain the problem. I suddenly realized he was drawing my dream of seeing inside of my foot. I was more than fascinated! I didn't say anything to the doctor but the minute he left the room I told Erv, "The doctor just drew my dream." +

I could tell in a few weeks that the culprit in my foot was gone. The incision was very sore, but the nagging pain inside had finally disappeared. Later, when talking with my mother, I learned that I didn't walk until I was nearly two years old and no one could understand why.

During my recovery, one night when in one of those states that I call half asleep and half awake, I suddenly saw, felt, and realized in a unique way, that there was a fluorescent-like light running through my body. It started at my toes, went through my foot, up my leg, through my trunk and right up to my brain. + I didn't know what it was, but I knew all was correct and was flowing through my body. I knew for certain that my foot was going to heal. Later when explaining this unusual event to my friend, Sylvie [a chiropractor and acupuncturist who had

16

administered acupuncture during my foot problems to help relieve the pain], I traced where the light had appeared to be. She replied with surprise, "You just traced the acupuncture line from the brain to the foot." I knew for certain that Spirit had indeed been speaking to me.

Lying in bed for a month was not easy, but I did it with more confidence knowing that this time the problem was finally going to be over. Watching the leaves pop out and hearing the birds sing as they greeted spring helped.

For two years I had been mostly home bound and had done massive amounts of reading. I felt almost spellbound reading one of my favorites, *The Power of Myth* (an interview of Joseph Campbell by Bill Moyers). This book created a renewed interest in my spirituality and a new quest for the meaning of life and my place in it.

I read the entire book *Course of Miracles*, which is a self-study development course that was dictated by a clear inner voice to Helen Schucman, from 1965-1972. The writings deeply resonated within me and awakened in me numerous questions. I began to realize that Spirit could communicate to us today in many ways, just as in Biblical times.

I read several books on dreams, and then I began to tackle scientific and medical books. I was disturbed when I read that it might be possible for individuals to bring on their own illness. I knew I was still trying to figure out why Pam had gotten so ill. Why was I having foot problems? I became extremely interested in patient/doctor relationships and in the role a person should play in their own health. I was trying to find answers to difficult questions.

I ventured into reading about alternative and holistic practices. I was intrigued in reading *Joy's Way* written by Brugh Joy and learned about chakras (energy channels). Chakras are invisible energy vortices that penetrate the human body and body aura. Joy explained this huge network of energies throughout our body. Chakras are believed to play a vital role in physical, mental, and emotional health. His writings helped explained the strange sensations I had felt when I laid my hands on Pam's face.

I became engulfed in the book *Man's Greatest Gift to Man*. It is the life of D. Palmer, a magnetic healer, who discovered chiropractic medicine. He explained how nerve impulses in the body have to be perfectly balanced in order for the body to work perfectly. Organs that do not receive normal nerve impulses undergo functional and organic changes. When the relationship of nerve impulses are disrupted or reduced they can become diseased. Illness results. He explained how he could feel these nerve impulses, (subtle energy). His words helped explain the light I had seen go from my foot to my head. His words also provided a deeper understanding of my experience of laying hands on Pam's face.

After reading dozens and dozens of books, I felt better knowing that the mind, brain, nerves, body, environment, genetics, and food all contribute to the disruption of perfect body function; consequently disease can take over when all is not in harmony. I was learning that for perfect performance, the link between intelligence and matter must be 100%. The link between the brain and the nervous system in the body has to be working perfectly in order for the body to work properly. I still didn't understand all of the disruptions that caused my foot problem, Pam's illness, or Deanna's problems, but I better understood the complexity of the situation.

Three surgeries later, I was more enlightened. I now knew the importance of the balance of the body. I felt even stronger than before that everything in life can be a lesson. We either become bitter, or we grow from each experience. My foot troubles had slowed me down. God had given me an opportunity to take a closer look at my life: to learn more about life and my place in it. I know I learned the lesson that illness can be a gift from God. With pain comes wisdom. I now better understood if you want to gain eternity you must serve your time. Physical suffering is an opportunity to gather treasures for Heaven. I had felt depression and sadness, but also wonder and joy at my newly found peace at being alone with myself. My faith was advancing to another new dimension.

Amidst all my personal activities our extended family began to grow. On September 2, 1992, we were blessed with a grandson. After eight years of marriage Joe and Kathy had Alex, a big, healthy, wonderful bundle of joy. And I mean a big bundle. He weighed over ten pounds and the size of his hands and feet went off the charts at the hospital. Alex inherited plenty of tall genes. Kathy's father was six feet six inches tall and Joe is six feet three inches. By six months Alex weighed over thirty pounds and looked two years in size. At ten he was five feet tall.

(In 2010 he was 6 feet 5 inches.)

At the end of October, I was invited to give a talk on death and dying to a group of schoolteachers at a Mid-West Teachers Conference in Kansas City. When I finished my talk a woman in the audience asked if I'd written anything other than about my daughters' death. I told her I had a collection of interviews with several dozen unwed mothers and I thought their stories would be very helpful as a sex-education book, but I wasn't a teacher and didn't know how to go about writing a book for a classroom. A woman in the back of the room held up her hand and said, "I'd love to help you with that project." I suggested we meet afterwards to discuss it. When we met, Di immediately said, "God sent you to me." + my insides stirred and I knew this was going to be fruitful.

I explained to Di that in the seventies I helped start an organization for unwed mothers. Our organization had helped more than 500 young women, and I had kept in touch with many. During this time, Erv and I had opened our home to five young women (at different intervals) who needed a place to stay during their pregnancy. I'd recently interviewed these women plus others. They all shared their feelings on how they now felt, after twenty years, about relinquishing or keeping their child. I felt that their experience and sorrows would help a young person contemplating sex to become more responsible for their decisions. Di agreed. She asked me to mail the interviews to her in Kansas, and she would compose lesson plans. We would meet later to put our thoughts together.

Often I heard from Di, that things were going well in the classroom. Her lesson plans were complementing my interviews and the students were very interested. She suggested I add interviews on AIDS, and if possible question the fathers and parents who had been involved. She kept saying, "I'll find the time for us to meet." Months passed. I got more interviews, and she came to town for a short time. We knew we needed to spend a length of time together but when and where?

Then a phone call in the latter part of October informed me Di was in the hospital. She had fallen and broken her hip. I couldn't believe it, as she was only forty years old. My heart went out to her knowing the confinement and months of rehab that were ahead. I had just gotten out of that cycle. Deep inside I hated to admit it, but I wondered if God wasn't at work again to make us find the time. God messages seem to come in all avenues, and this time it was her turn to slow down.

In about two weeks she was out of the hospital and called to say, "I'm coming to Columbia. I can recuperate as well there and I think God sent me this accident so I would slow down and get this book done." + I acknowledged that had occurred to me but I didn't want to say it.

We spent an intense week working together. We became great friends. Friends of the heart. We enjoyed working together. We both understood, "No one can stop anything God starts." We felt His constant help. Everything just seemed to fall into place. After our time together I spent many hours typing and putting the material together. Within a few months, through a series of +'s that I won't go into here, we found a publisher. He told us, "If you put this together as a teacher's manual and a workbook, I'll publish it."

With son Joe's guidance and my Macintosh, I put together what Mr. Hollis requested. It was months of work, but since I still had a tender foot, it gave me something to do. The fruits of my labor paid off and we had our work published. (*Now and*

Forever, the Responsibilities of Sex, Accelerated Development, a division of Taylor & Francis, 325 Chestnut Street, Philadelphia, PA)

***

Also during this time, when I was able to get up and about, a friend asked if I would like to take a Bible Study Class at the University of Missouri. Since I had been doing copious amounts of spiritual reading for months it sounded like a + to me. My friend worked out a special place for me to park to accommodate my limitations. The class I attended was an Introduction to the Old Testament, taught by Professor Greggs. Never did I read the Bible so much and so closely. I was expanding my knowledge of religion and gaining many new insights. Integrating religion, medicine, and science was crowding my mind. I was yearning to know it all.

Once the professor gave an assignment to write a paper about our truest self. In order to begin, I began asking myself questions. What is my truest self? Why was I born? What is the meaning of life? From where did I come? Why am I here? Where do I fit in? What's it all about? What is my role? Then I began to write:

***

I think my quest for life, my search, my purpose, and trying to understand God and what it's all about is the deepest part of me. I love the warm intuitive feeling I get when something is just right and I know it. That sense of being in tune with what is and what is meant to be. To reach and touch that inner core that tells you it's right. To me that's being in touch with God. One has to be keen to their intuition, their gut feelings, to stay in touch with what is going on in the universe.

Life with its distractions can add to or subtract from this. It's all in how we perceive and handle each situation that in the long run makes us become what we are. We are the result of exposure from our parents' example and teachings, from many teachers, from a spouse if married, from those we associate with (friend or foe), from what we read and see, from life in general. It's our reactions and how we respond that makes us truly what we are inside. I like to think that each happening in my life, small or large, sad or joyful, is an opportunity to grow. My life is its fullest when it is full of love. I think through love our spiritual life grows. My spiritual growth is of utmost importance and through this I hope to attain eternal peace.

***

I received a big "A" on my paper with a note from the professor that said, "I've never read anything this profound in all the years I've given this assignment." I swelled with pride and knew I was growing in my spiritual quest.

My insides, my soul, my heart, all felt different after the expressed realization of who I was. I realized that we can all reach this inner feeling, inner knowing, by searching, reading, gaining knowledge that nourishes the soul so that faith blossoms. Over time, faith can and will blossom like a flower, if one works at it. But we have to nurture and nourish our faith constantly. I was learning how to trade off what I thought I should do for what I felt God wanted and expected me to do. It was definitely another turning point in my life. It felt like a new beginning. I vowed to continue to nurture my faith.

December 8th, 1992. I had what I call a profound dream. In this dream I learned to fly. In the dream I saw a lady, hanging from a balloon-like object, flying overhead through a spacious field. I called up in the sky to her, "Help me, I want to learn to fly." Suddenly I realized a child was there to help me. The child was carrying a lightweight pink blanket, and by fluffing it up, it resembled a balloon. The child kept encouraging me to grab hold telling me I could fly with it. I wasn't having much luck when all of a sudden a bright chariot appeared in the sky. As it flew by, individuals in the chariot began depositing little packages on the ground. I raced from one box to another, to see what they contained. The boxes had "Happy Birthday" written on them. Inside the boxes I found herbs and seeds that I knew I had to plant. I thought, "If I can see a chariot come out of the sky, which is unusual, then surely I can fly." Suddenly, I was about two feet off of the ground, flying around with the child. I could see lots of people flying, low and high, but I was afraid to go higher. Then I saw an angel, hovering over a huge tree and knew, "I've got to go to the angel." All of a sudden I was high and looking down. I flew and flew. I felt like I was flying over the world. At one point something tugged at my leg. I looked down, and a little dog was hanging onto my leg, flying with me. The small child caught up with me and sat on my shoulder and we three flew together for what seemed like hours.

When I awakened, it was with a sudden jolt. I felt like I landed. I got up to go to the bathroom and my feet felt heavy. Whew! What an experience. It had felt wonderful. This dream certainly got my attention and I knew I would always remember it. It felt like a + and I wondered about its deeper meaning.

The Gift of the Light

I received a phone call from my good friend, Patsy, who lived in Atlanta. "Nancy, have you heard about the apparitions of Mother Mary going on at Conyers, Georgia? I've been a few times, and all I can think of is you when I'm there. Why don't you come to visit me and we'll go together." She certainly piqued my interest. I've been intrigued with apparitions since childhood, when there was much interest in the messages from Fatima. I remember how then I was jealous of the children who saw Mary, the Mother of Jesus.

Since I also have a brother Greg who lives in Atlanta, I decided to take Patsy up on her offer. I called Mom in Kentucky to ask her if she would like to go along to see Greg. I kept thinking of my Aunt Martha (my mother's sister). I called to see if she would also like to join us. I drove to Kentucky, picked up the two of them, and we went to Georgia. Mother decided not to go with us the next day to Conyers. Martha and I were up at 5 a.m. to meet Patsy and the three of us were on our way. We were excited about our upcoming adventure.

Martha, Patsy, and I arrived at 7am, May 13, 1993, to a crowd of 1000 or more already assembling. We'd heard the apparition generally took place around noon. We were able to obtain a good parking place, which apparently is very hard to come by. An attendant parked us right in front of the yard where the apparition takes place. + My feet, still weak and achy, were grateful. I told my companions, "It certainly is starting out well. It is probably going to be an interesting day.

We placed our portable aluminum chairs strategically in front of the apparition dwelling (which was already five or six rows deep with seats and people). We then joined in the long line that was quietly, reverently, and prayerfully proceeding through the apparition room. Only certain invited guests remain in the structure during Mary's visit. I was trying to get into the spiritual feel but couldn't. My mind was clouded with lots of doubts.

We then proceeded to roam the grounds, seeing the grottos, visiting and obtaining water from the well, which we had heard had caused some miraculous cures. We proceeded to a place called the Holy Hill, where a volunteer had built an altar with a huge crucifix.

As we knelt in front of the altar Patsy said, "Now, be serious. I understand that when one prays from their heart here, their prayers are answered." I silently prayed, "God, if it is true that Mary is appearing here please send a sign to help me to know and believe." I wanted to believe but everything inside me was saying this might be a hoax. I also said a prayer for Deanna, eight months pregnant, who was having difficulty. Deanna's doctor had told her, from viewing weekly ultrasounds, that the baby was laying sideways, face forward. The possibility of the baby choking on the umbilical cord at delivery was strong. I prayed and pleaded, "God, I don't think Deanna needs any more sorrow in her life. I know I certainly don't. Please, bless Deanna with a healthy baby. She's already lost a baby with a tubular pregnancy. It's time for my daughter to have something good in her life."

Later the three of us stood in line to obtain free books, that explain the mysterious apparitions, and lists the messages she has been receiving since 1987 from Jesus and His Mother. On the 13th of every month Mary gives a public message to Fowler to give to the people of the United States. (The 13th of the month is also the dates Mary appeared at Fatima in 1916.) Close to noon, when the apparition was to take place, we returned to our chairs. At the time there was a light sprinkling of rain. Martha, who had been snapping pictures all morning, reloaded her camera. My camera remained in my purse as I had decided to try to get into the experience instead of busying myself with taking pictures.

Nancy Fowler had arrived and was in the dwelling. Fowler appeared to be a very simple woman accepting her call in life that was obviously creating a big stir. I understood that when she receives the message from Mary she relates them quietly to her friend George, who announces them to the crowd over the loud speaker. I heard that only she sees Mother Mary, but I read that sometimes others present in the room see a bright light, smell roses, and experience profound feelings.

A few minutes before 12:00 noon, the crowd that had now swelled to over 25,000, circled the building, and began to pray and sing in unison as the darkness of a storm began to roll in. Lightening was streaking the sky, and all were very aware of the ominous clouds above. I am altogether fearful about storms and could not believe I was sitting here on a metal chair, holding an umbrella, as if asking to be struck by lighting. I was scared and shaking inside. I generally run for shelter in my basement when storms are apparent. It was getting darker and darker. Then, slowly, from the distance, a bright, different, lone, white, cloud slowly moved into position over the roof of the dwelling. The crowd was praying the Rosary. (An organized prayer that is simply walking with Mary through the life of Jesus.) There was a spectacular bolt of lighting and thunder. I shook inside and wondered if we were about to witness something profound. It briefly entered my mind that it could be the end of the world. It was so dark. Then I saw another bolt of lightning, that seemed to be inside the white cloud, and simultaneously, it was announced that Mary had arrived. The rain stopped. We continued the rosary.

Then it began. The unexplainable, indescribable, rotating, white clouds, that hung over the dwelling, outlined by the dark ominous clouds, gave a spectacular display. To me, it was like a kaleidoscope revolving and turning, mesmerizing me. I was seeing faces, Mary and Child, images, angels, etc., in the cloud movements. I asked Martha if she could see what I was seeing when I noticed she was already snapping pictures of the clouds. I felt that if I let go of the arm of my chair that I was gripping I'd float up to them. Then directly overhead, in the midst of the dark clouds, there began an ever so slightly opening to expose a distant sun that appeared unusually tiny. Many individuals were shouting, "Look at the sun, look at the sun." Martha continued to snap pictures. To the naked eye the sun seemed to change sizes.

Soon the message from Mary was delivered to the crowd. +*"Dear children of America, the time has come for you to respond to our invitations of love. Please children wake up, while there is still time. You are going deeper and deeper into the darkness. Again I say to you, if you refuse the peace of my Son, then you will be at war. You will have war between nations, in your communities, in your families and within yourselves.*

On this anniversary day, I ask each of you to recommit your life to God. My children everywhere, join your hands and your hearts to God and to each other..."

Shortly it was announced that Mary was leaving and departing from the apparition chapel. I heard over the speaker, "She is rising to the ceiling, she is going through the roof." Then an almost tornado rush of wind swirled the trees near the roof top, and the crowd was showered with thousands, and thousands of catkins, the little snake like hangings from the oak trees. Immediately this was followed by another tremendous gust of wind and the crowd was showered a second time with the oak hangings. A phenomenal sight, which brought all eyes in a different direction, to suddenly see another unbelievable cloud display. Clouds were coming out of the ground. The clouds rose upward in a swirling, rotating, feathering, climbing, motion that lasted several minutes. It was unexplainable. It was beyond belief, but I was seeing it happen.

Then the rain began to pour. It was a drenching downpour. Water and mud rushed down the hillside where we sat. Yet, all of the spellbound thousands remained and continued praying the entire three mysteries of the rosary.

As Patsy and I crowded closely together under one umbrella, in the downpour, I asked, "Would you have ever thought, twenty years ago when we met, that the two of us would be in this position? Sitting in the rain, under an umbrella, in the middle of nowhere, at an apparition site, praying the rosary?"

When the three of us returned to the car we began sharing our feelings and experiences. We were on a high and filled with wonderment. We discussed at length how we all had experienced an unusual sense of peace, joy, and love among all those attending, and hadn't felt the presence of a huge crowd. We couldn't get over the fact that we were dry and no mud.

I commented, "When insights such as this happen and have the feeling of goodness, truth, and honesty, they create an inner awareness that demands I pay closer attention. Little did I expect that my childhood interest in apparitions would return with such velocity.

I felt I had not given the place the credence and reverence that it deserved. For me, it had been dramatic, mysterious, and mystical. The fabulous miracle I witnessed was a captivating experience for its audience of thousands. I knew my prayer on the Holy Hill had been answered. I'd been given the sign that the apparitions here were true. + There was no doubt in my mind that Martha was supposed to be there as my witness and my photographer. The experience had been captivating, profound, and not of normal reality. The demands of the experience prompted a response from me. I knew that I would return.

Close to Greg's home we took Martha's film to a one-hour photo. When we picked the pictures up a couple of hours later we were thrilled. The developed film confirmed the sightings in the clouds and the unusual sun occurrences. The most spectacular picture was a bright light outlining Mother Mary ascending amidst the swirling trees. There were several pictures in the cloud formations that depicted Jesus, Mary and Child, a man with his arms out-stretched over the crowd, angels and many more. The four different pictures of the sun were startling to see because Martha had never changed the setting on her camera; but the sun definitely took on different distances and sizes. In the final picture, there was a large cross in the clouds, with a heart and cross in front of Mary as she departed. (I found out later that this is exactly how the visionaries in Medjugorje, Yugoslavia see Mary depart. She has been appearing daily to five individuals there since 1981.) (Pictures on my website- www.nancymertzlufft.com.)

That night God wouldn't let me rest. I began to experience a very unusual array of light images while trying to go to sleep. It started with a likeness of the sun appearing and disappearing, but it seemed like images were speeding by an inner vision plane that I couldn't describe. Also I kept feeling a prompting of words to say. + I couldn't turn this off in my mind and I decided God wanted me to write what I had witnessed that day. I got up in the dark looking for paper and pencil. I wrote an eyewitness account of our visit. When I lay back down I witnessed more floating pictures of light that I couldn't distinguish. It was like panoramic objects were flowing in front of me as I lay with my eyes closed. The images weren't clear and I wondered if they could be saints, or angels. In viewing this light, I was feeling much confusion, and wondered why this was happening to me. Was I going crazy? I've read enough about dreams to know and understand that I wasn't having a lucid dream, nor was this a figment of my imagination. No drugs, no alcohol, no hallucinating. I was definitely awake and experiencing something unique and inexplicable. I prayed for the Holy Spirit to enlighten me. I eventually fell asleep.

The next day I told no one about my night experiences. It seemed too weird and I was afraid they might not believe me. We drove back to Kentucky. I called Deanna to see how she was doing. She informed me that she had gone in for her third ultrasound that week and the doctor had remarked, "I don't know how but the baby has turned and is in the birth canal." + ("Thanks, God, for another prayer answered.")

Heavenly Text

That night I stayed at Mom's in Kentucky. Again, when I went to bed, I started seeing the lights. + I saw and felt what I thought was an earthquake. I felt fear, anxiety, confusion and sadness. I became frightened and wondered if we were going to experience an earthquake in Kentucky, but something inside of me said, "No in Missouri." I knew Missouri has one of the worse fault lines in the world. Was there going to be an earthquake? I was very confused. I finally went to sleep. (I now think God was telling me my life was going to be going through major changes-like an earthquake.)

The following day, there was a get together of about thirty family members, since a nephew was celebrating a college graduation. I was excited about my recent trip and was sharing with everyone my enthusiasm and my pictures. It didn't take long for me to realize I was alone in my excitement. They did not believe me. I was shocked. I was glad I hadn't mentioned the lights that I had seen at night. There were lots of doubt, suspicion, and actual comments that let me know building credibility was needed. I knew it wouldn't be easy to convince this group.

On the way home from Kentucky I stopped to see my foot doctor in St. Louis. I had been seeing him the last three months because my supposedly good foot had been giving me lots of trouble. I was taking massive doses of an anti-inflammatory, and at night wearing a brace from the knee down. My foot wasn't getting better, and the doctor said he hated to, but he was going to have his nurse give me a shot of cortisone in the plantar fascia of my foot. He said it would be very painful, but he didn't want to let this go any longer. My right foot was acting similar to the early problem stages of my left foot. He said he was trying to prevent another surgery.

The nurse came in and apologized profusely about giving these shots because they were so painful. I was scared, but relaxed and began to silently pray, "God," I pleaded, "I went all the way to Georgia to see Mother Mary. Please be here with me now, as I really need you. I'm scared." The nurse gave me the shot. I hardly felt anything. + It was more like a tiny, tiny, pinch. The nurse remarked, "You are the best patient I've ever had for this procedure." I smiled and remembered how Pam had often said that her treatments did not hurt when she put them in the hands of God. I promised God that for six months I would investigate Marian apparitions to help build credibility for them (alleged sites visited by Jesus' Mother).

Several days after I arrived home another unusual occurrence: I was sunbathing on my deck. I was lying on my stomach with my eyes closed, when I realized I was seeing an eyeball, a living eyeball with movement, with the lashes blinking. My first thought was, "How can I see my own eye here on this towel? It's not a mirror." I knew my eyes were closed. I opened and shut them several times and each time I closed them I could see the eye, with lashes blinking. It was "a living eye." + It intrigued me and as I viewed the eye I asked, "Who does this belong to? I'm confused. Why this? I'm afraid." The occurrence lasted only a short while.

I spent the first few days home reading the books written by Nancy Fowler. The writings are messages she receives from Mary and Jesus. A very unusual thing happened while I was reading a statement from Jesus, *"I send many signs to my people - Many in the form of nature. Even a bird can be a sign from me."* + At that instant, a bird appeared at my window next to where I was reading, scanning up and down, as if trying to get in. I was startled, and at first a bit fearful. I fell to my knees and gazed at the bird. I had never seen one like it: the bird was brown with a yellow chest. The bird eventually stopped its motion and perched on a branch not a foot from me. From the branch it was looking directly into my eyes, turning its head from left to right, staring at me. The bird stayed there looking at me for some time. I trembled and shook, began to cry, sob, almost paralyzed with wonderment, feeling a deep profound sense of God's presence. The supernatural atmosphere that enveloped me was intense and intimate. I felt one with nature. To me it was +, confirming to me that the messages were real. I had asked for a sign and here was another. I was in shock. I began to recall a lot of the same feelings I had experienced when Tiger, our cat had returned.

I immediately called Erv but he wasn't in his office. When he arrived home for lunch I was still very shaken from the experience. When I told him what had happened he said, "Nancy, don't ever tell anyone that story because they will truly think you have lost your mind." I knew right then that my work was going to be an uphill battle.

When Erv went back to work I called Father Mike Quinn, the pastor at the Newman Center, where we attend church. I said, "Mike, I really need to talk to you. You won't believe all that is happening to me." I guess he heard the anxiety in my voice and said, "I'll be right over." We've known Mike for years. He had at times said Mass at our home when Pam was dying.

When he arrived, I explained everything; the apparition site, the eye, and the bird visit. He was very kind and receptive. He shared with me that his aunt had been to Conyers and she had told him she saw Mother Mary when she was there. He was thrilled to hear another affirmation. He gave me his aunt's name and suggested I call her.

Mike and I talked a lot about St. Francis talking to animals and he assured me that God created everything and everyone. We spoke of how birds in myths often function as celestial messengers. I shared how I've always been intrigued by birds and that as a child I had scrapbooks of bird pictures. We decided that God speaking to me via a bird was perfect, because He speaks to each of us in our own unique way.

When I told him about the Lights, he talked about how many people down through the centuries have talked and written about visions. He said, "Maybe God is trying to send you visions." He suggested I pray whenever I saw the Lights and ask for God's help. If they weren't from God they would go away.

I explained how I needed to go back to Conyers. That I

had promised God for six months I would try to write and add credibility to the apparitions. I explained how I was confused but thrilled. I didn't understand why the church doesn't talk about or endorse them. I wanted to help people understand. I was going to try to gather lots of information. I was becoming aware that there is much negative talk about "Marian people" and "Marian devotions," as if this group was a separate segment of thought in our church.

I read that Nancy Fowler asked Jesus why there are messages from Mary and Jesus explained. + *"I give the world my love. I also give everyone in the world, my dear, Holy Mother. Please, if you accept my love, then how can you reject, ignore, not honor, not love, My Mother. I come through My Mother and I want you dear children to come through My Mother on your journey back to Me."*

I shared with Mike that I had read all the messages given to Fowler and they were about peace, love, faith, repentance, conversion, prayers, and fasting, which are certainly in line with our faith. Many of the messages and prophecies were somewhat frightening, and seemed to be in accordance with the Book of Revelation. I didn't totally understand all but if I believed part of this, I guess, I was going to have to believe all of it.

Mike suggested we meet and talk if unusual things continued. He suggested I try to relax, to let God lead me, and see what happened. He wished me luck. I felt much better after our visit.

In thanks to God for all of my new gifts I started attending daily Mass.

I continued to have occasional nights of seeing the Light, not knowing what I was seeing. I thought often about Pam and remembered her saying, "I see Christ's Light." I just prayed and prayed, asking God if these lights were from Him to please teach me and help me to understand. I told no one accept Erv and Father Mike. I wasn't about to share this strange information with others. The fear of what others would think really bothered me. I had tried but couldn't even get my children interested in the subject of apparitions, much less something like this. I well remembered all the doubts and misgivings I had before I had made my trip. I hoped time would take care of everything.

I began to read about many apparitions. I read about old ones, to the present ones taking place all around the world. There are over 300 places where people claim to be having apparitions at this time. I wondered why we never hear about them at church. It should be exciting news that the Mother of Jesus is coming to help us.

The apparitions in Medjugorje, the most famous apparitions, have been going on for over twenty years. Many books have been written about Medjugorje and millions of people have visited the site. I understand that Mary has said Medjugorje is like the hub of the wheel of all the apparitions going on in the world, and when they end in Medjugorje, they will end everywhere.

I was thrilled when I heard from others who had been to Conyers or to Medjugorje. One day a couple that I had not met before came to see me. Someone I knew had told them about my pictures and they wanted to see them. They had seen an unusual occurrence in Medjugorje.

The man, a medical doctor, shared his miracle story. He told me he considers himself an intelligent man - that he knows he was not hallucinating when he saw the cross on the hill at Medjugorje (a cross anchored in concrete) spin in midair. Several other people witnessed the event at the same time.

Aunt Martha called one day and said she had learned that a daughter of her friend was in Conyers on the same day we were. The daughter lived in Nashville. She had taken the exact same picture of Mother Mary departing on May 13th. This young women's group also witnessed a rosary turning to gold while the crowd had prayed. I've also met several other people who were at Conyers in January and March. One person had her rosary turn gold; another had a cross turn gold. The credibility was building with all these strange happenings and events. A friend of mine was going to go to Conyers in June, and I hoped to go again in July.

On June 13, 1993, exactly one month after my visit to Conyers, Deanna had a healthy baby girl. They named her Kristine Pamela. To me, Kristine was a gift, brought by Mary, on this special day of the thirteenth. It was strange that Deanna's doctor had scheduled Deanna's labor to be induced on a Sunday. When the doctor realized what she had done, she tried to change the date, and was informed by the hospital there was no way to change the date because of conflicts in the maternity ward. For me, this was a confirmation that my second prayer on Holy Hill had been answered. +

At Conyers on this day, my friend reported no unusual occurrences. She had heard from others that scientists were there, testing Nancy Fowler for authenticity. She said the crowd was very large. It was reported to be over 80,000. She advised if I planned to go in July to go early.

On July 11, 1993, a friend from St. Louis, Anita, went with me to Conyers. We stayed in a motel within 30 minutes of our destination. On the morning of the 12th, we arrived at the apparition site around 10am. I was amazed to see, a day early, so many cars already present. I was even more amazed when we were parked in exactly the same parking spot + as in May - An excellent place right next to the apparition site.

A huge crowd was expected the next day. People were already placing their chairs around the building in anticipation. We took our chairs to find a place. The row of chairs already placed, indicating where to place the next, was in exactly the same spot where Martha, Patsy and I had sat before. + I commented, "This is eerie! First the parking spot now this."

We then spent about thirty minutes in the apparition room. Again my body was jumpy, I felt unsettled, and it was hard for me to pray. I couldn't seem to concentrate. We then proceeded to the Holy Hill. I felt more reverent this time, as I had grown in my belief of the real presence here.

That afternoon the visionary, Nancy Fowler, stood on her porch and spoke to the crowd of several thousand and answered questions. I gave her a copy of the pictures Martha had taken in May. She said, "Jesus has asked me not to comment on pictures." She looked at them. She then smiled at me and said to her friend, "George, show the crowd the pictures. " + Sounded like a confirmation to me.

That evening we watched the news. We saw five scientists being interviewed who had been present at the Conyers' apparition the month before; and had performed tests on the visionary in order to scientifically prove or disprove her credibility. They explained that Fowler had been connected to electrodes to measure brain wave patterns before and during the apparition. One of the doctors reported that the EMG showed that during the apparition she had changed instantly, from a stressed state to a highly relaxed state. One doctor reported an EEG went crazy. Another machine measured magnetic forces, to determine significant energy forces. Still another machine emitted beams of infrared light, which help detect presences not seen by the human eye. All of the scientists said that the tests showed Fowler was not hallucinating, was not having seizures, was not hypnotized, but had to be in a supernatural state because the readings at the time of the apparition showed that by all signs she should have been dead. I was thrilled to hear the first credible apparition news I'd ever heard from the press.

Something prompted and awakened us early on the13th. We dressed and arrived at the apparition site around 6:45am. As we pulled into the parking lot I noticed the guard in my rearview mirror putting up a barricade, indicating the lot was full. We were one of the last cars to enter. We were parked in exactly the same spot as before. + In fact, the man strangely parked us in front of other cars where it would be impossible for them to get out. To think, out of thousands of cars, the same wonderful spot three times. When I say the same spot I mean within ten feet. There were just too many happenings to be coincidences. + I knew, "God wants me here."

Anita and I separated and spent our own quiet time. It was around noon when we rejoined each other at the chairs we had put up the day before. It was extremely hot, over 100 degrees. There were lots of people, lots of thermoses, and lots of umbrellas for needed shade. Again the crowd was very reverent. No spectacular storm this time. And the rain would have definitely felt good.

As the crowd said prayers, waiting for the arrival of Mother Mary, I scanned the sky with my camera looking for unusual clouds. I wanted more pictures. Without warning, I instantly saw in the camera lens, an object that moved toward me. As it got closer, I suddenly realized I was seeing an image of Mary. + I caught a slight glimpse of Jesus' Mother, via my camera. The occurrence was quick. I totally came unglued. I shook, I cried, tears flowed from my innermost being. I felt honored, I was thankful, I was astounded, and I was shaking so much I couldn't even take a decent picture. It's impossible to put into words how I felt. It was a profound spiritual experience. I was exultant with a unique inner joy. I looked away from the camera and looked up in the sky and I saw nothing. They then announced Mother Mary had arrived.

I had asked for a sign again and God was sending me signs left and right - - this time, the biggest of all. I kept wondering again why I seem to fall apart. Later, Father Mike said to me, "Maybe that's ecstasy."

The Blessed Mother Mary remained for almost an hour as the crowd of over 100,000 prayed three rosaries in the sweltering heat.

The message was heard: + "*My dear children, open your hearts to God and allow my Son, Jesus, to live within you. Surrender your will to His will. When you do this, you will have peace and direction for your life. My Son desires to heal each one of you. Go to Him. As my Son loves you and forgives you, you are being called to love and forgive each other. Pray,*

Heavenly Text

little children, pray. Express your prayer in love and in this way you will have a closer union with God. "

Anita and I were glad to get out of Atlanta before rush-hour traffic. On the other side of Chattanooga, as I was driving down the mountain highway, I internally heard, *"Slow down, Nancy."* + Instinctively, I started braking. Immediately, we rounded a curve and witnessed two semi-trucks turning over. I truly felt the warning had saved us from the terrible accident. We had missed being involved by seconds. As the truck drivers were climbing out of their overturned cabs, I was able to go around them by driving through the island in the middle of the interstate. We felt extremely lucky. We knew traffic was going to get backed up for a long time. Later we heard the interstate was closed for twenty hours.

North of Nashville, we decided we were tired, and started looking for a place to stop. We found a motel and were told, "It's our last room." + There was an amazing feeling that luck had definitely been on our side the entire three days. ("Thanks, God.")

Unbeknownst to me, a neighbor and her daughter also decided to go to Conyers on this same day. I had shared with them my experiences of May. During this apparition they had sat next to a woman and her 10-year-old daughter. My friends learned, that some months before, the daughter had experienced a miraculous cure at the site. She had been cured of a strange skull formation that caused frequent infections. The child had had the condition since birth and after her first visit to Conyers, her routine MRI showed no problems. Her doctors were very surprised and puzzled.

When my friend's daughter asked her if they came to Conyers often, she was informed that they come every month. My friend asked her to share some of their experiences. The woman said the most dramatic by far was in May. She proceeded to tell them about the unexplainable rotating clouds that contained visions. My friend told me that her daughter's

38

eyes got big with amazement as she said, "Mrs. Mertzlufft was telling the truth."

After this trip to Conyers the clarity of the Lights at night seemed better. I tried to relax more instead of fearing them, and the pictures were clearer. I started noticing that before they would begin, unusual warmth would creep over my entire body. Sometimes I would experience a jerk or a jolt. The Light most often began with what appeared to be clouds, opening and shutting. Then a circle would appear. It was like I was looking through a telescope. The circle would grow bigger and I could see pictures inside it like a video. I reluctantly started calling them visions.

One night I saw a vision of flooding. + I didn't understand where. I saw a house floating in water. Soon after that, copious amounts of rain fell in Missouri. The big flood of '93 resulted. Days later I saw on the front page of our newspaper a picture of a house floating down the Mississippi river. I was stunned. I ran to the other room exclaiming, "Erv, this is exactly what I saw in a vision: A house floating in water - just exactly like this picture. I know it's exactly the same. I can hardly believe it." It was a very weird feeling, knowing I had been shown a future event. Seeing this helped affirm that my visions were coming from God.

A few nights later I experienced a vision of seeing Pope John Paul II. + I saw his face get closer and bigger. No doubt it was him. I then saw a gun pointed towards him. Then I witnessed him being shot. I saw a man running from the scene. I was shocked to be seeing the occurrence that I knew had already happened. Or was it going to happen again? First a future event. Now a past event. I was feeling very strange and uncomfortable that this could be happening to me. I've heard many negative comments about psychics in my life and I didn't want to be considered one of those.

The next month, on August 13, 1993, I scheduled my time to be home, out on my deck, at noon. I thought, "I'll pray and view from my deck here in Missouri, because we all have the same sky, sun, and heavens. Who knows, maybe I'll get another glimpse when Mary's on her way to Conyers."

In my lounge chair, I felt silly with my camera in hand, but I prayed and talked to Jesus and Mary, sort of reliving the two months I'd been in Conyers and wondering what was transpiring there. I remember praying; "I know you are here in the United States on this special day. I know you're everywhere, not just in Conyers. I'll snap a few pictures of the sky and clouds just in case you're passing by." I saw nothing unusual.

During that night, + while praying and experiencing images in a vision, I was suddenly brought to reality with a strong jolt. I heard an audible voice distinctly say "**Write**." + It was a human voice, as real as my own. I was awake. I know I was awake. I know I heard a gentle voice say, "**Write**." No one was in the room but Erv and me. Erv was asleep. First visions, and now voices. I wondered if God wanted me to write about my visions. I remembered it was the 13th. Was it Mary I heard?

It was about three weeks later before I had the film developed that I had taken on my deck. When I picked up the photos I was stunned. + God had indeed given me another gift. Jesus was, in the photo, looking down at me above my rooftop. How special and honored I felt. I was in awe. I immediately called Aunt Martha and shared with her. She asked me to describe the picture. I said, "Envision a male face looking straight at you from above the rooftop. His face, eyes, mouth, mustache, are all there in a subtle way. It looks like a spirit overlay. There's a pinkish glow to the left side of His face and it looks like the silhouette of Mother Mary. There's a cloud formation in the sky that resembles the shape of a map of the United States. Streaks of light from the sun radiate throughout the whole picture." ("Thanks, God.") (The picture is on my web site - nancymertzlufft.com)

Aunt Martha later sent me the message from Conyers for August 13. A friend had sent it to her. The crowd had been estimated at over 90,000. Approximately fifteen minutes before the apparition, a perfect a cloud formed a cross over the site. It remained for a lengthy time. Chills ran up and down my spine when I read that Fowler said, **"Today the face of Jesus appeared, superimposed over His Mother."** + The description sounded like the picture I had taken on my deck.

For a couple weeks after I heard the voice there were no more Lights, images, or voices. I missed them. Every night I prayed for guidance and asked God why they had stopped. Then one night, when almost asleep, with my eyes closed, I suddenly witnessed and saw a dramatic bolt of lightning. I felt frightened, really scared, and I wondered if I was being reprimanded. All the next day I kept thinking possibly it was a scolding for not following through and adding my visions to my writings. Then the next morning my Bible seemed to just open to Matthew. Chills passed through my body as I read, "What I say to you in the dark, tell in the daylight; what you hear in whispers, proclaim from the housetops." (Matt 10:2) I felt guilty. I was embarrassed for not proclaiming them. I was struggling with self-confidence and unworthiness.

A few days later someone gave me a book to read. + It helped in alleviating my fears of sharing visions. I felt lots better when I read in Wayne Weible's book, *Medjugorje, the Message*, that he too, had heard voices and had visions. It gave me confidence, like a partner in an adventure. I found it odd that I hadn't heard of his book before. How similar in that both of us were writing to prove apparitions. Weible's book certainly helps many people since he explains from his non-Catholic viewpoint.

Reading Weible's book gave me courage to tell a couple more people, good true friends, about the occurrences of the Lights. A big mistake! They were leary. Their doubts and comments made me feel uncomfortable.

September 12, 1993. I received a letter from Jane

Heavenly Text

Thibault, PhD, (a gerontologist and professor at the School of Medicine at the University of Louisville). She explained that she was using my book about Pam in her classes. She wrote. "I have found your book, *Gift of Life*, not only inspiring to me, but extremely helpful to my medical students, family medicine residents, and quite a number of our faculty. Would it be possible for us to meet?"

The arrival of her letter set me on top of the world. I felt proud knowing my book continued to help others. In response to her letter I had called only to speak to her voice mail. I thanked her, and explained that we were already planning to be in Kentucky the next week on our way to Florida, and to let me know if there was a convenient time to meet.

September 13, 1993. Patsy returned to Conyers. She reported no unusual occurrences. In Missouri it was pouring down rain so I remained in my house. I prayed the Rosary. While praying, with my eyes closed, I had an unbelievable number of visions, some with small amounts of color. It was like a video that flew by, and I could occasionally distinguish what I was seeing. I saw glimpses of Jesus. I saw drops of blood. I saw Jesus kneeling and thought I was possibly seeing His agony in the garden. Then I saw a figure standing with many people. I thought it was probably the scourging. I jumped up from my knees where I was praying, and went into the other room. I definitely was trying to escape. I later apologized to God for being so fearful. (Now, I know what a gift that was.)

September 14, 1993. As I sipped my morning coffee the phone rang. It was Jane from Kentucky. She asked, "Would you be able to speak to my class next week, plus a visit with me?" Little did she know that over the years, when individuals asked me what I had hoped my book would accomplish, I'd always answer, "I hope someday to speak to med-students. I think patient-doctor relationships are of utmost importance."

Jane and I talked for some time. She shared, "Through

42

you, I've come to love Pam dearly. I realize today is her birthday and I'll be speaking about her tonight when I'm giving a talk to some senior citizens."

(I thought to myself, "I haven't even thought about today being the anniversary of Pam's birth. Here a stranger is singing her praises, and reminding me. She really does know Pam well. Thanks, God.")

September 24, 1993. Jane was to pick me up at 8:30am I had spent the night at my sister's in Louisville. (Erv was on a three-day golf outing with my six brothers.) I had awakened at 5am. I lay with my eyes closed, thinking about what I was going to say to the medical students. As I thanked God for bringing me, an unusual vision suddenly appeared. + I was seeing a huge circle, that looked like a sun, vivid in oranges and reds, with the silhouette of a person standing in the lower right section of the circle. It was the first time I'd ever seen this bright of a color in a vision. I was fascinated and wondered what it meant. Something inside of me said, + *"It's going to be a fun day."* Little did I know how wonderful.

The minute I saw Jane I liked her. She was bubbly, enthusiastic, and sharing of herself. I felt an immediate kinship. As the day went on we both knew it was no accident that we were brought together. It was more like we'd always been aware of the other and had just found each other. We talked alike. We thought alike. We expressed ourselves much alike. We soon found out we write alike. We felt a spiritual bond. I was meeting a sister of the heart. God had truly brought us together.

My presentation to the medical students was well received. I could tell their minds were spinning with interest and wonder as I spoke. I explained the benefits of doctors being involved with their dying patients. I shared how death can have meaning, purpose, and be beautiful. I stressed how one has to embrace death in order to experience it, so that it becomes as beautiful as birth.

After the class we went to Jane's office. She was excited

and thrilled as a child when her secretary handed the final galley of her manuscript to her. She said, "What a perfect day for this to arrive. God sent you to be with me today to share in this moment. Pam has influenced my views on suffering and death. It's my first book. It's my baby." I easily recalled the feelings of joy I felt when I had received my final draft for *Gift of Life*.

Jane slowly opened the envelope, with almost a reverence, saying over and over how glad she was that I was there to share the moment. When we saw the beautifully designed cover and read the title *A DEEPENING LOVE AFFAIR, The Gift of God in Later Life*, tears welled in our eyes. To me, the cover reminded me of the picture that Jesus had given me in my photo. The cover of Jane's book was a picture of the sky at night with the moon; my picture is the sky in the day with the sun.

The feeling of the moment is hard to explain but we felt an unbelievable closeness of being partners in a writing adventure straight from God. We felt His presence. + Jane had written the step-by-step instructions, in how to find God within by listening to that inner calling. I was writing about my personal life as an example, calling them God Messages.

For me, a circle had been completed: Pam's death, my growth by writing and sharing, Jane relating to my book and using it in her classes, and now discovering that the two of us wrote similar books. God had brought us together to share in the knowing of our shared interest. What a beautiful example of the circle of life. I decided this moment explained my morning vision. I remembered that Jesus had told Nancy Fowler, *"Put the "O", a circle, from the word LOVE, around yourself, and make it grow, to your family, to your community, to the world. The bigger the circle grows the closer you get to Me."* + ("I'm feeling it God. Thanks.")

Later, Jane told me that her favorite part of my book was when in the hospital Pam stated that God talked to her. The night before, as I had prepared my talk, I had reread the same page, with renewed interest. I shared with Jane that I was receiving visions and had heard a voice, and that I now realized Pam probably had heard an audible voice. When Pam had originally told me God talked to her, I had thought it was probably a dream, or a deep knowing. Now I think differently. I've often wondered why Pam and I never spoke of that incident again.

Jane said, "I feel visions and voices happen to many individuals, and they are afraid to tell anyone for fear of what others will say. Afraid a doctor will say they are crazy. Or worse yet, institutionalize them." I confided, "You truly are a gift sent to me from God because I am feeling anxious about sharing that part of my life with others." She said she was having trouble, too, wondering what others would think of her. She gave me such strength, saying over and over, "Do you realize how much God loves you? He loves you to death, or this all would not be happening to you."

I knew God loved me, but until she uttered those words, I had been operating more out of my love for Him. I was performing and carrying out my life in the way I thought He wanted. I hadn't dwelt a great deal on the thought of how much God loved me. Her words gave me a renewed peace.

It was fabulous finding us comrades, supporting each other. I told her about Tiger coming when I received Pam's book. She remarked, "God sent you 'Tiger' the day your book was published. He sent me 'you' on this, my day." It was truly a day of delight, love, fun, and a feeling of oneness. It was as if our minds were one in thought.

At 5pm she dropped me off at my sisters. We parted knowing a close friendship of the deepest kind possible would be ours for the rest of our lives.

As I drove the next hour to Mom's I thanked God over and over for the wonderful day. Mom and I spent a relaxed evening talking because the guys were on their outing. I was bubbling over telling her about Jane, our likeness, and the similarity of our journeys in life. Somewhere in our conversation I told Mom about the visions I had been receiving. It upset her. She uttered, "I'm worried about you. Are you going crazy? Are you all right?" I assured her I thought I was fine and was sharing everything with a priest.

Then to my amazement she shared, what I would call, a life-long secret. "I never even told your daddy this. I thought he would think I was crazy. But thirty-seven years ago, the day Chris [one of my younger brothers] was born, something strange happened to me. I had a vision." She proceeded to tell me in a very picturesque fashion, using her arms to describe what she saw. I was in awe and delight. I felt a penetrating closeness to her. It was interesting to me how the circle had come around from mother to daughter. We'd experienced sameness and now the circle was growing because of my writings. I told Mom, "I know that visions are a gift - given by God. They are His communications with us. I'm learning to grow through them. Thanks for sharing yours. It makes me feel better."

Two days later, on our way to Florida, Erv and I stopped at Conyers. I could still feel Erv's skepticism. For months he heard me talk of practically nothing else and had observed my constant writing. He had agreed to go with me to Conyers if it was a non-apparition day. He didn't want to deal with a huge crowd.

When we arrived, I suggested we say the stations, which are placed along the tree line surrounding part of the property. Fowler had asked Jesus to explain to her the best way to pray the stations that are pictures depicting the sufferings of Jesus. I had forgotten my glasses, so as we walked the stations I asked Erv to read Jesus' recommended prayers. At the seventh station, Erv read: Jesus says, + *"Look at my eyes; see the love, compassion, the forgiveness, the hope. Never give up. I am where your eyes are. I am there looking into your eyes."*

I trembled. I was humbled and enlightened with an unexplainable knowledge and realization that the eye I repeatedly had been seeing, when my eyes were closed, was Jesus watching over me. + A profound gift. I recalled, "If

thine eye be single, thy whole body shall be full of Light."
(Matt 6:22.) "Thanks, God."

We prayed at the Holy Hill, visited the well, and attended
a prayer service, which is held on Sunday afternoons in the
apparition room. There were only about twenty-five individuals
present. In all we stayed about three hours. I again had felt
God's presence in an inexplicable personal way, as if His
angels were following me as I walked about.

During our stay, Erv remarked, "This place is more quaint
and rustic than I expected." I responded, "That should make
you realize, even more, that it's not the place that draws me
here. For me, it's the atmosphere that creates a sense of
knowing that this is all real."

That night I had a strange vision. + I kept seeing a bunch
of circles, like balloons, all connected. I couldn't figure out
what I was seeing but I felt as if I was inside this bunch of
look-a-like-balloons, and couldn't get through the mass of
them.

The next week when Erv and I were at Epcot Center at
Disney World, we were viewing a movie on the functions of
the body. I was startled when suddenly before me on the
screen there was a picture of the cluster of balloons that I had
seen before. I chilled and remarked to Erv, "I saw that in a
vision just the other night." I understood in viewing this video
that the balloon look-a-likes are the hypothalamus gland in our
body, but I couldn't imagine what that meant or had to do with
my vision. (It was seven years later that I read: (The activation
of the hypothalamus is the Universal Translator, and translates
all spiritual messages. Many messages are complete with
emotions, pictures, and language. The hypothalamus also
provides one with the identity of the sender. One will learn to
identify the senders after receiving for a while.) (Author
unknown)

I heard from Aunt Martha that a lady she knew went to
Conyers on October 13, 1993. I called and asked this woman

what she had experienced. She said, "I went to Conyers with some friends. I didn't expect anything to happen to me. I was just happy to go. I've just recently started going to church since my husband died. I'd not gone to church for over thirty years. When we were touring the apparition room a gentleman took a picture with a Polaroid camera. When the picture had developed the man was in awe, sharing it with others. It was very unusual, not a picture of the room we were in but it looked like a black cloud, with Jesus in the middle, with His arms outstretched. I was fascinated and surprised something happened that I experienced first hand. Later, I sat on a bench at the Holy Hill for a long time. I observed many touching the feet of Jesus on the cross statue. As I was leaving I also went up and touched His feet. It startled me and I jumped. The feet felt like flesh to me. It was like touching my own foot. I felt my finger make an indentation. I was surprised because I thought the foot would be hard. I said nothing to my friends. The next morning at breakfast we were all discussing the previous day. I remarked how surprised I was that the statue was soft. My friends informed me that it was made of wood and felt like wood to them. I was stunned. Since I've been home I've thought about it often. I know how it felt to me."

A cousin from Massachusetts called to tell me she had spoken with Aunt Martha, and had a name for me of someone who had a miracle at Conyers. My cousin worked with the lady's son, a Mrs. L.

When I called Mrs. L. she was very cordial and happy to share her story. She and her husband had just returned from the October apparition. She informed me that they go as often as possible. Mrs. L. told me that before Conyers she had had ulcerative colitis for twenty-five years, having uncontrollable bowel movements. In February of 1993, she had her yearly physical and colonoscopy with her family physician. He informed her she had diverticulosis and suggested she return to the surgeon that he had previously sent her to in 1983 for a colonoscopy. Before the tests she was required to take several enemas. Her son had suggested she use the holy water she had obtained from Conyers for her enema. He told her he had an inner knowing or feeling that she should do this.

The surgeon performed the test, which her doctor had requested and remarked that her colon was clear. He was even curious as to why her doctor had sent her. Mrs. L. reminded the doctor that she had previously visited him and he had diagnosed severe ulcerative colitis in 1983. The doctor didn't feel that was possible because she had absolutely no sign of ulcers or scars. He explained he would be able to see signs if she had this condition for that length of time.

They asked him if he believed in miracles. He checked his records and agreed that he had previously diagnosed her with severe diverticulitis and there was not a medical explanation for her new recovered condition. She had total recovery. He also told her he would be happy to document the cure for an inquiring investigation if that was necessary to prove the authenticity of the miracle.

Mrs. L. then shared with me her recent visit to Conyers. She said, "The scientists, physicians, and psychologists who had performed the diagnostic tests on Nancy Fowler were present and gave testimony to the crowd of thousands. The five doctors said they believed in the authenticity of the apparitions. One of the doctors said he had been a professed atheist before the testing and now believed in God and was reading the Bible daily. Another doctor stated he had been an agnostic but now believed in God. None of the doctors had known each other before the testing. They also reported that they had tested Nancy and another visionary simultaneously, and the unusual readings were exactly the same for both of them."

What good news for me to hear. A miracle, plus the scientists and physicians' public endorsements. Both certainly added more credibility.

(In 2010 Nancy Fowler disassociated herself from the organization that promotes money using her name at Conyers.)

Heavenly Text

In the *Noetic Science Magazine* I read where Brendan O'Regan, M.D. had collected data on people in remission of terminal illnesses. He discovered varying degrees of cures and remissions, some he called miraculous healings. He had learned that some of these cures happened at apparition sites that he had never heard of. He traveled to Lourdes and Medjugorje to observe and try to explain these occurrences. Afterwards he commented, "There is much to be learned from people in remission and people who have been healed in a spiritual way. They are, I think, the resource for the future. There must be a healing system within us that can, when triggered appropriately, recognize and eliminate cancer and many other diseases. The mind is certainly involved, albeit in a highly complex and varying way."

Back in July, when Anita and I were in Conyers, we had spent time talking with a couple from New York. They had informed us that they had been to six places in and out of the country where apparitions were taking place. They told us how impressed they were with Father Jack Spalding in Scottsdale, Arizona. So when I heard Father Spalding was coming to St. Louis, I knew I wanted to go meet him. The date of his talk was to be October 30th, which coincided with the end of my six months in trying to build credibility for apparitions. The date seemed more than a conincidence. It was perfect.

October 30, 1993. It is a two-hour drive to St. Louis. I was up and on the road by 6:15am. I was anxious to meet and hear this priest speak about the apparitions going on in his parish. Father Spalding gave two one-hour talks in the morning. His talks were interesting, but not once did he mention the word apparition or anything about them. One talk was on learning to grow from our crosses in life. In this talk he explained that if there's something one doesn't understand that's probably their present cross. The second talk was on the difference between worry and concern and how to handle both in our lives. Again, nothing about apparitions. I was confused.

Why was I here? I came for apparition comfirmation and was getting none. I figured the majority in attendance were probably were here for the same reason.

During the break I spoke to the lady sitting next to me. I discovered she goes to Arizona for the winter months, and attends Mass at Father Spalding's parish on a regular basis. She informed me that the bishop forbade Father Spalding to speak about the apparitions outside of his diocese. (So, his hands are tied by church authority.)

At another break, Father Spalding was available for short individual visits. The line was long. When I finally came face to face it seemed only appropriate to make the statement, "I'm concerned that you're my cross." He naturally looked startled. It was hard for me to try to explain in two minutes all that was on my mind. I'm sure I only confused him. But then, I too was confused. I tried to explain how frustrating it was to be writing about apparitions, under Jesus' watchful eye, and not experiencing endorsement from the church. I explained that Father Mike had supported me, but that was about it. I had hoped for more confirmation and affirmation from him for my fact-finding mission.

That evening, as I drove home I kept asking God, "What am I supposed to write about this experience? I feel you sent me to see this priest. Why?" The more I thought about it the more I felt God was nudging me to address the fact that the church does not endorse His Mother's visits to earth. It is well known the church has always been prudent before offering a position or judgment concerning apparitions or miracles. I question why. It appears to me the authority of the church seems to be threatened by what it cannot explain. It seems that church authority only wants to approve within its inner circle the evidence as researched from within, and everyone else is suspect. I wonder what gifts and enthusiasm of its members the church loses because of doubt and silence. It is a pity the church does not offer psychological support for its seers. It appears to me that the church is more political in its guidance rather than supporting its followers.

Heavenly Text

Weeks later I was able to obtain a video, *I Am Your Jesus of Mercy*, (The Mercy Foundation, P.O. Box 8141, Scottsdale, Arizona 85252-8141. Proceeds are given to charity.) that explains the apparition in Scottsdale. I viewed the video with extreme interest. The professionally filmed video gave me needed information and comfort. Father Spalding fulfilled my wishes on the video by answering all of the questions I had wanted to hear in St. Louis in October. I learned that the apparitions began in Scottsdale in 1987 with Mother Mary appearing to a young woman, Gianna Talone, who is a member of Father Spalding's Friday night prayer group. Talone started receiving apparitions after visiting Medjugorje. She alone sees Mary, but others in the prayer group have experienced visions, locutions (internal messages), and other profound spiritual happenings. This video certainly added credibility and made me feel not alone in my recent spiriutal experiences.

In watching the tape I also realized the extreme differences of apparitions in Scottsdale and Conyers. I learned that God is for all, the rich and the poor, and that the way we respond to His call is what is important, no matter who, what, or where we are in life.

I also learned that sometimes when delivering his sermons, Father Spalding is sometimes used as a speaking vehicle for Jesus. Father goes into an altered state of consciousness and Jesus speaks through him to his parishioners with words of love and comfort. Some would call this prophecy while others might call it channeling. This occurrence appeared very genuine on the video.

Also, on the video was a quote from the bishop of the diocese explaining that the church does not necessarily endorse the apparitions in Scottsdale, but if the apparitions were causing more people to pray, merit was being served.

Watching this video made me feel even more strongly that the stringent criteria for accepting miracles needs to be changed. I believe the church is God ordained, God inspired, and accomplishes its work through its members. That's why I have taken the initiative to try and -- prove the authenticity of apparitions in my own way. I believe that our faith should not be crippled by the inexplicable or be blinded by the beauty of the spiritual realm. When I went to Conyers out of curiosity, filled with doubt, I was shocked and surprised. I had to let my faith take over. I had to get out of the way and let faith be my guide. To me, faith means letting my mind trust God, my heart respond to the love of God, and my will submit to the commands of God.

For six months, I had witnessed and been a part of spiritual occurrences that were previously foreign to me. What I encountered had drastically changed my thoughts, my life. I knew that it was true, that Jesus was calling us through His Mother. The Light had lured me by the magnetism of the Holy Spirit. I realized God had reached into my dreams to prepare me. My life was mirroring my dream of seeing the birds place blossoms on branches. I was in essence purging myself, sharing my spiritual encounters. I believe the other dream of the lady teaching me to fly was preparing me to see and write about Mother Mary. That dream did occur on December 8, which is a feast day of Mary in the Catholic Church. At the time, without realizing it, I was shown via dreams; an opportunity for growth would be presenting itself. I vowed that in the future I would record all of my dreams. I now knew God was the abiding source of Light in my life and in my dreams.

I believe the doubting of my family and friends helped to spur me on to continue to do research and write. I strongly felt the need to prove to myself and to others that what was happening at Conyers was real. I drew strength from reading dozens of books, especially *Discernment,* written by a theologian, Morton Kelsey: "We realize that we are not as simple as some people would like us to be. By looking back over one's experiences, one can see that we may well be in touch with another realm of reality which is different from that of the senses and the physical world.

To experience the depth within, and in this way discover

the depth of another reality, takes time and effort. One has to learn the way by trying oneself. The church once knew how to approach this other reality. But the church has been so taken in by the materialism of the 19th-century science that it not only rejected its own practice, but then forgot that humankind had any need to deal with the realm of the spirit. It is clear that one often has to start all over again, often without the church's guidance, and counselors have to try out and know the experiences themselves before they can guide others. As with matter of experience, one can lead another no further than one has been oneself."

My searching was also a continuous prayer to know Jesus and Mary better. I now know and believe that Spirit is trying in multiple ways to open hearts and minds to a higher knowledge. The Catholic religion believes the Eucharist is the body of Christ. Is an apparition any more of a mystery?

Jesus began His thoughts with His apostles. Little by little His mind was their mind, because His influence became theirs. His thoughts became their thoughts. His words became their words. Hopefully, my thoughts and words are what He now wants.

November 4, 1993. I had a vision. + It was a dark scene. I saw a huge moon, a large gorge with running water between some mountains. I saw a "black cat" on the mountian top. The cat was trying to get down to the running water. I remember wondering if this deep gorge had resulted from an earthquake. I had never been afraid or superstitious about black cats. In fact, our family owned a black cat at one time in my life. I was confused.

(Much later, I decided this vision was explaining that my unconscious was mysteriously taking me to a deeper canyon of my mind so my thirst would be quenched.)

November 13, 1993. Another vision. + I saw what appeared to be a long tunnel. I could see the image of a human figure at the other end. I felt peaceful, as I seemed to go towards this image. I remember wondering if this tunnel resembled the one people talk of going through in near death experiences. Why was I seeing this?

(Now, as I think back, I think this picture was telling me my future was going to be like going through a tunnel. Also, possibly, God was sharing with me that I was working on my entrance into heaven.)

I read a tremendous amount of books as I wrestled with understanding visions and how to better explain them. The more I read, the more enlightened, yet the more confused I became. It was refreshing to know from Scripture that visions and dreams were common in Biblical days. I knew Jesus had visions at His Baptism, in the desert, at the transfiguration, and in Jerusalem and we don't call Him hysterical or crazy.

Jane also helped me to better accept my visions by sending me the wonderful book, *The Interior Castle* by Teresa of Avila. St. Teresa's writings helped dispel my thoughts of being alone concerning the Light, the visions, and God Messages. Her words and descriptions resonated perfectly. This book helped me understand I could go on with my life, learning to accept what God was bestowing on me while learning what He expected from me.

Towards the end of November in a vision, I saw a circle object. At first I thought it was a coin, or a large host. + I could see a clearly embossed fruit symbol on it. Then I saw a casket with someone lying inside. I could not distinguish who the person was. I wondered if it was me? I also saw an infant's long baptism gown draped over the front end of the casket. I was very confused and wondered if someone I knew was going to die.

(Much later I realized that the Host represented Christ-- The Fruit of Life. Like a new baby I was receiving new ideas of believing.)

Heavenly Text

Another night I had a vision that was very different from any previous ones. I could see Erv and myself in our family room. + I seemed to be viewing both of us from above. It was strange to clearly see myself. Viewing the scene felt uncomfortable. Erv and I seemed to be arguing. I saw myself stand, I saw myself fall. I couldn't distinguish enough to totally understand what was transpiring.

Later, I realized this vision was preparing me because at times our relationship would become difficult. Erv just couldn't relate to what was happening to me. My life was changing drastically and he didn't understand.

I often wondered what I would have thought and done if the experiences were happening to him instead of me.

During December I had two visions in one night in which I briefly saw Christ. + The first was a glimpse of what I thought was Christ's face. I was elated. The scene passed quickly. I thanked God over and over, and prayed I'd be able to see more clearly. Then another vision appeared and I saw a distant scene of Christ on the cross. + This scene faded away and I saw a hand bleeding. I knew it was Christ's hand with the bloody markings from His crucifixion. I questioned, "Why this? Am I going to go through sufferings?"

Later, when talking all of these visions over with Father Mike, he remarked, "Maybe, the messages of this past month are all about life, death and communion. You are experiencing new thoughts on life and death."

Now, I know his statement was right. It's easier to look back now and understand this was when I was dying to self. What some would call the-dark-night-of-the-soul.

With the passing of months I better understood that all my visions in November and December were warning me of the times ahead. I was going to be sharing in Christ's sufferings. Not physical sufferings but sufferings of the heart. I had experienced six exhilarating months and now unbeknownst to me, I was destined to spend six frustrating months.

Heavenly Text

The winter months seemed to put me into depression and hibernation. My life took an abrupt change. I was consumed with trying to understand and piece together everything that was transpiring. I gradually dropped out of old activities because they weren't fulfilling a need. I felt out of the circle of conversation and ordinary life. No one seemed to understand where I was coming from. I couldn't talk about what was going on without getting negative responses and I couldn't fully enjoy myself because I was more interested in researching my new thoughts. I just faded away from my old life style.

I could also tell my thoughts, my knowledge, and my confidence were slowly growing. Through many readings I had discovered there are many viewpoints regarding mind and body, soul and body, health and disease. I knew there were levels of God knowledge, many levels of scientific knowledge, and I wondered if and when all would ever come together. I was gaining knowledge but it was hard to assimilate it all. I was trying to simplify a very complicated topic for myself.

I began questioning my thoughts, my ideas, my sanity, and myself. It was strange at the time, and even stranger to write about it now. As I look back it seems that before each new horizon I had to weather a storm before the burst of joy. At this time in my life I just lost my courage. I was feeling down and overburdened with non-support from my family and friends. Tension was building deep inside.

Even though I'd received gift after gift, I doubted myself. I wasn't able to share and talk with others. I was reluctant to share out of fear; of what others might think and what consequences it would bring. I was relaxed with Father Mike, Aunt Martha, very few friends, and sometimes Erv. I'd always shared everything with Erv, but was finding myself more reluctant to even share with him because he wasn't sharing my enthusiasm. It was easier to keep many special moments to myself because I didn't have to deal with any doubt or concern. I'm only human and being ridiculed or made fun of wasn't easy. I was full of gloom and doom. Hearing words of skepticism and doubt had made me more and more reluctant to talk about what was going on in my life. I felt isolated and alone.

I knew deep inside that if someone could read my life, from beginning to end, a different picture would be painted. I constantly was asking myself, "Why am I embarrassed?" If and when I did share with someone, I often caught myself saying, "Now don't tell anyone else just yet. Let's keep it between us. Wait until my writings are totally finished." Afterwards, I'd be so mad at myself for making remarks like that. Why couldn't I let go of fears about what others thought? I was bold enough to be writing about my experiences, but not bold enough to share them. I seemed to be caught in a circle and couldn't make myself get out of it.

At social gatherings, whether it was happening or not, I felt that behind my back comments were being said, "Have you heard, Nancy thinks she's found a special relationship with God, and calls it God Messages," or "Did you know Mertzlufft believes that Mary stuff." It disturbed me knowing I could not be everywhere to explain "ALL." Another part of me just wanted to hide.

I now realize I was learning that I couldn't change others' hearts and minds. No matter how much I loved Erv, my family and friends, I couldn't prove what I was experiencing or convince them. And that was the hardest. I wanted to do it for them. I thought I could convince anyone, that everyone would believe as I did. It was hard to come to the realization that each person has to evolve in their own way, on their own schedule. No one can do it for another.

In the process of hurt and frustration I found myself beginning to go within with the pleasures of the experiences of God, instead of becoming more aggressive, which is more in keeping with my style and nature. I continued to write, but found I was becoming less and less verbal publicly. Ultimately, I was trying to understand what God expected of me and how I was to go about broadcasting what I knew to be true. I guess one would say I was wrestling with witnessing.

In essence, I was shutting out as much as being closed out. Inside me a storm was building, and I felt I could explode. An eerie feeling had me in its grip. Only God knew how uptight I was. I even made a trip to my doctor complaining of restlessness, anxiety and off and on heart pains. I explained to my doctor that I had experienced several nights of very rapid heartbeats, and I wondered if I was going to have a heart attack. My doctor put my mind at ease with an EKG.

Now, I know without a doubt, this was the time God was trying to enter deeper into my heart. It was a difficult time. I had been forewarned in visions, but never made the connection until much later when I read *Spiritual Passages*, by theologian Benedict Groeschel. Groeschel wrote of individuals experiencing inexplicable physical symptoms when entering into a deeper relationship with God. He referred often to God reaching further into one's heart.

It was months before I pulled out of the depths I felt would never leave. On Easter Sunday, April 3, 1994, I received a wonderful gift. It lifted my spirits beyond expectation. When I awakened I could hear the birds singing. Spring was in full force. As I lay with my eyes closed, I began to feel the warm familiar glow that precedes my visions. It had been months since I'd had a vision experience. I was elated. I was startled and stunned when the brightness of the Light intensified. Suddenly I saw the spirit of Mother Mary. + She was standing, all aglow, with a blue white light radiating intensely all around her. I gasped, and whispered, "It's her, thank you God, what a wonderful Easter present." I saw many angels kneeling in adoration. I felt an unbelievable joy. I felt blessed. It's impossible to put into words the feelings of bliss. The scene faded.

I immediately shared with Erv that I had just seen the spirit of Mary. He made no comment. I was bouncing with joy. I could hardly wait to tell Father Mike at Mass.

After this my life seemed to pick up and I began feeling better. My visions picked up. My visions continued at different times throughout the night. I had no way of controlling, accepting, or rejecting them. They just appeared.

Heavenly Text

April 10, 1994. + I started seeing a bright circle object that I thought was the sun. There was a dark cloud under it. This scene repeated at least a dozen times. I internally heard, *"I'm with you, do not be afraid although the times seem dark to you."*

April 13, 1994. + This vision began with large eyes, with beams of Light streaming from them. Not once, but many times the vision was repeated. I felt tremendous peace. I felt I was receiving grace. It was Mary's special day of the 13th and it felt like a thank you for writing about apparitions.

April 15, 1994. + A very clear vision of an eye. This time I saw a tear running out of the corner of the eye. I watched the tears run down the side of a nose. I saw no other parts of the face. Then I saw what looked like a battlefield with combat taking place. I had a strong feeling of dread and destruction. I questioned if this was depicting the warfare going on within me. Was Jesus or Mary shedding tears of sadness or tears of joy?

April 19, 1994. + I saw a group of people walking. They wore oriental hats. Suddenly, there was a huge flash of light. I saw a mushroom cloud form and knew I was witnessing the explosion of an atomic bomb. I began to cry and was frightened. I prayed this was a symbol for me and not a future occurrence. Now, I know it was preparing me for my next vision: a huge explosion in my life.

April 21,1994. A profound experience. I was embraced by the Light. + Truly embraced. I had awakened and knew Erv had left for work. (Erv usually gets up around 5am.) With my eyes closed, I was just lying in bed saying my good mornings to God. I began experiencing the warmth, but this time it seemed to be more intense. I was seeing movement of clouds, the flutter of wings and the light that often precedes a vision, but no pictures came. This process must have happened a half-dozen times. I wondered as the clouds opened and shut if possibly I was going to see Mary or Jesus because the feeling was so intense. It was a feeling of empowerment, warm and gentle. Then I saw the warm, alive eye, penetratingly looking at me, with streams of Light coming from the eye to me. I knew it was Jesus expressing and demonstrating His love to me. I thanked God for the extra grace He was showering me with when all of a sudden I was hugged. It was a strong, meaningful, compassionate hug. I felt arms around my body and immediately opened my eyes because I thought Erv had returned and was hugging me. I was in bed alone. I felt the tightness of the hug, for a few more minutes, experiencing the Light at the same time. My entire upper body felt surrounded by arms. I quivered with emotion. Then it was over. I lay there in awe with tears flowing from my eyes. It had felt so personal and private.

How was I going to explain this unusual, wonderful event? I feared no one would believe me, but I knew no one would ever convince me it didn't happen. All day I kept reliving the moments trying to recreate the feeling of the experience; it had been so overwhelmingly nurturing. Over and over throughout the day I prayed, "Thanks, God. You outdid yourself. I don't deserve these shows of emotions. How profound they are to me. How grateful I am Jesus, to know you're truly here with me. I adore you."

I didn't tell anyone about this vision for days but kept it to myself as a special treasure to relive over and over. I feel strange typing and sharing now because the experience was so special, yet I think God wants me to share it. A few days later, when reading scripture, I don't think it was an accident that chills abounded + when I read, " On my bed I think of you, I meditate on you all night long, for you have always helped me. I sing for joy in the shadow of your wings." (Psalms 63:6-8)

In prayer the next day, I had an interior knowing that I was supposed to look up the meaning of the word "adore. " The dictionary said, "to worship, to venerate, to praise, to glorify." As I pondered on this I had a sense, a knowing, that the word

61

adore could be equated with the feelings of a mother for a newborn baby. I asked myself what those feelings were. As a mother I cuddled, I kissed, I hugged, and I gave unrelentingly of myself in love and attention. I was consumed with trying to mother a helpless infant, so dependent on me. I felt needed.

To think of being loved and needed by Jesus, as a mother loved her child gives me comfort. It's how I now perceive His love for me. He is protecting, cuddling, and reassuring me as I continue to do His will. I had felt His presence. I felt His love. I felt His need for me. I know He wants me to adore Him. I feel He wants and needs me to do His work. He never tires of my questions, my comments, my pleas, and my love. He needs me just as I need Him.

April 22, 1994. (Father Mike had asked me in 1992 if I would take communion to a man named Bill Gardner. Mike knew that since Pam's death I had adopted the charitable work of taking communion to nursing homes and home bound individuals. On the first day I met Bill my heart melted and I visited weekly until his death in 2002).

On this day I went to visit Bill at the nursing home. He was a very intelligent man who was born with cerebral palsy and 90% deafness. After his parents died he came to Missouri to study for a master's degree at the University of Missouri School of Journalism. After completing his master's degree he obtained a job with the Cerebral Palsy Foundation here in Missouri. On his way to work one day in 1990 he fell on the ice and is now a quadriplegic. He has no use of his arms and only uses his legs to transfer in and out of his wheelchair. He has no close family and he has no money. He was placed in the nursing home by the state in1992 when the trust his parents had set up for him had been depleted.

This day Bill was expecting me for the pizza lunch we had planned the previous week. Upon my arrival he explained that his hearing aid was not working properly. So I fed him in silence.

There is no way to describe the pleasure I witnessed that

day. As I cut the pieces smaller and placed them into his mouth, he made noises of glee straight from his heart. Something so simple as a pizza, that I so take for granted, was sending him into ecstasy. He was reeling with emotion and it radiated from him. I knew the true meaning of the words: "When two or more of you are gathered together I am with you."

As I left, I gently gave him a hug of his face and witnessed tears of gratitude that gifted my heart for hours. I am rewarded with warm feelings from him often, but this day had been special. +

April 23, 1994. I received a phone call from Sandy, a young person in her thirties who I knew through church. Sandy wanted to know if I would take her to see Sister Breige McKenna, a nun who has the gift of healing. She shares her story in *Miracles Do Happen*. She was going to be in St. Louis on the evening of April 29. Sandy informed me that Sister Breige was a nun healed instantly from crippling arthritis and now had the gift of helping to heal others. Sister gives talks and is an instrument of God's hands as she goes out into the world delivering God's word.

Sandy was hoping that by going to see Sister Briege she would receive further healing from her multiple back problems. I had met Sandy the year before, when I took communion to her home while she was recovering from back surgery. She still had many problems. Sandy said she had received permission from the priest of the parish in St. Louis to bring a chaise and lay down during the service.

I don't particularly like to drive at night, so I told Sandy if she were willing to spend the night in a motel I would take her. Maybe the trip would be beneficial for me as well, because my feet were still not totally normal.

April 28, 1994. Father Mike had asked me to take communion to another new patient in the hospital. His name was Jay. When I saw Jay the clarity of his eyes and manner surprised me. He looked better than I thought he would, since I had been told that, because of an accident he was paralyzed from the waist down and recovering from brain injuries. He had been in a coma for six weeks. He was ever so slowly regaining his mental abilities. He could not talk, but something in the way he gestured to me when I gave him communion gave me a profound sense of his awareness of God on a deeper level. +

While visiting him, his mother arrived. I told her that I was going to see Sister Briege the following day and I would pray for their family. She handed me Jay's guardian angel pin and said, "To help you not to forget."

April 29, 1994. + I awoke to a beautiful vision. Loving eyes were radiating streams of Light to me. Internally I heard, "*Trust Me, trust Me.*" + I knew it was going to be a good experience to see Sister Briege that evening.

Sandy and I left for St. Louis about 2pm. During the two-hour trip we talked about healings. Sandy confided that what she really wanted was just to touch Sister's hand. She felt that would make her happy, and give her strength to be more accepting of her condition. We checked into the motel, had an early dinner, and went to the church around 6:15pm. We were lucky in finding a close place to park.

When we entered church the usher took us behind the altar and placed Sandy's chaise in front of the music group. Sandy was upset about the placement saying, "Sister's back will be to us when she talks." I had the sense + we were in a good place and told her, "Just relax, I think this is perfect." Sure enough, before mass started, Sister Briege came out and sat directly four feet across from us. We could see her perfectly for the entire evening.

Sister spoke on the importance of believing in God's presence in the Eucharist. During the sign of peace, I walked over and shook Sister Briege's hand. She commented, "Tell your friend I'm praying for her." I turned around and Sandy had gotten up, walked over, and was shaking hands with Sister

Breige. Sandy and I were two out of only about six individuals that were privileged to give the sign of peace to Sister. There were about 1,000 in attendance. I whispered to Sandy when she returned to her chaise, "See, you got your wish."

After Mass the priest celebrated benediction. A host was placed in a monstrance, which is a vessel in which a consecrated host, the Eucharist, is placed and exposed for adoration. The priest walked among the crowd, with the monstrance, giving blessings. When the priest stood in front of Sandy and me, he lowered the monstrance down to where Sandy lay and blessed her with the sign of the cross. The power, the strength, the feelings that radiated from the Host was powerfully intoxicating. I felt an inexplicable power and intensity, much like during my embrace. I felt the outpouring of God's grace. I was praying that Sandy was experiencing the same.

Later that night in the motel we shared our thoughts of the day. Sandy told me how the power of the host in the monstrance had astounded her. She said she had never felt anything like that. I shared my embrace story. Sandy then shared that as a convert she had never totally believed in the true presence of Jesus in the host but she certainly did now.

The next morning when we awakened, Sandy immediately asked, "Did you have anything exciting happen to you during the night? Visions, anything?" I shared that I had experienced the same vision several times, but I didn't have the foggiest idea what it meant. + I explained that in the vision I saw a circle of light that looked like a cartoon character. The circle of light seemed to have a small tail of light on its bottom; a smile on its face, and it seemed to bounce from one place to another on the tail of light. The light was by a bed, by a chair, in a crowd, watching others, driving a car, just bouncing around. I reminded God during the vision that I didn't read the funnies in the newspaper, so a cartoon character wasn't a very good way to communicate with me. I confided to Sandy, that I didn't know if I'd ever figure out the vision's meaning.

On the way home Sandy said, "I'd forgotten that I brought

some tapes for us to listen to on the way. They're by Sister Briege. Would you like to listen now?" Naturally I agreed, and she passed them to me from her reclining position in the back seat of the car. I put a tape in the cassette player. Sr. Briege's talk was on intuitiveness, my +. I felt she was speaking directly to me. Sister stopped in her talk at one point and said, "I'd like to say a prayer right now for all those having trouble witnessing. " She began praying, "Help all those who are your little lights out working in the world.... " + I burst out with tears, chills, and said, "Sandy that's it, that's what the vision was showing me last night. God was trying to show me how He sees me. Literally bouncing around, smiling, and doing for others." It was a profound moment. A big, big, + overwhelming me with joy. I was elated. I knew God was confirming my writings and my work for Him. I cried tears of joy the rest of the way home.

As I dropped Sandy off at her home and gave her a hug, she replied, "I'm so happy for you. I know it's what God was telling you."

I arrived home floating on a cloud. Erv greeted me with, "Were your feet healed?" I replied, "Nope, but I had a healing." I knew God had given me courage, more reason to trust and believe, and lots of grace. He had given me His blessings.

I was home only a few minutes when Erv brought in the mail. I received a letter. I had previously sent for literature from an apparition site that I'd recently heard about, at Our Lady of the Snows in Belleville, Illinois. I had heard that a man, Ray Dorian, was receiving messages from Mother Mary on the 13th of every month. I was hoping to go and check this place for more apparition credibility. I was thrilled when Erv told me he would go with me. We decided to go the next month.

This literature explained that Ray Dorion had experienced apparitions of Mary for a little over a year. When I read of this man's determination to pass the messages on and not to worry what others said, I knew that he understood what reluctance was all about. Maybe he could help me. I wanted to meet him.

One of the messages I read that Mary had given to Ray rang straight into my heart. +"*With love all things are possible, and without it, you cannot share your accounts of your experience to others. You cannot be lukewarm with your love for me....*

The second message on witnessing in one day. + I was thrilled. I just had to call Jane in Kentucky and share my enthusiasm. I shared how I thought God was finally helping me with courage. She exclaimed, "It happened for me this weekend, too! I've been fighting this embarrassment thing. Why can't I enjoy talking about my book? Then there was a review in our local paper. I about died when I saw it, knowing everyone would now know I wrote *The Deepening Love Affair*. I wanted to crawl in a hole until I read the review. The reviewer described my book as a written exhortation. I looked that word up in the dictionary, and when I saw exhortation meant 'eager encouragement from a different dimension,' a feeling of complete relief filled my bones."

We both rejoiced together that simultaneously, God had given us a newfound courage. A newfound trust. Jane remarked, " God might not be giving you a physical healing, but He's healing our souls. " I agreed.

The next day, I made a trip to the hospital to take Jay back his guardian angel pin. I had worn it the evening we saw Sister Briege. When I handed the pin to Jay, he clearly said, "Thank, you." + One of his first words since the accident. It was another extra special moment. It was as if God used me as a messenger of healing via Sister Briege. Jay's mother and grandparents were present and the tears of love and joy I witnessed made me feel exuberant. My heart was overflowing.

After visiting Sister Briege, thoughts on healings were constantly on my mind. As far as I was concerned I had already known many healings in my life and expected more because I was learning to look beyond physical healings.

I now believed God, the physician of all healings, distributes healings in many different ways. For instance there is the healing of accepting loss. Through Pam I've learned to accept death. Pam was not healed of cancer, but all of us who knew her were healed in accepting her death. **This is the healing of relinquishment.**

The healing of my heart when I answered the question "What is my truest self?" I've learned to love deeper and trust more through +'s. I feel I belong to God above all else. Whatever He asks of me I am trying to carry out. **This is healing of self**.

The healings associated with my foot problems continued. My foot was by no means totally cured. I still wore tennis shoes most of the time, but I thanked God I could walk. I had not mastered physical healing as I had good days and bad days. I did know I was healed mentally in many ways with this experience because I learned **the healing of solitude.**

I grew spiritually and emotionally through visiting an apparition site. I grew because of God's special gifts. These gifts from God were transforming me. My daily reading of the Bible helped me learn a piece of my heart each day. I no longer relied upon myself but on God alone "who takes care of everything." **This is the healing that comes with faith**.

When my visions started I was scared. I didn't understand. Why me? As time goes on I'm learning to accept visions as God's words in my life. I seem to gain a deeper knowledge each time a vision occurs. **This is the healing of the fear of the unknown.**

I also am learning the **healing of my mind**. I am learning to feel comfortable in writing about a subject many will question. I agree with Cardinal Newman who once said, "The more a man is drawn to God, the less the world will understand him." I feel God's constant presence urging me on. I feel wiser, more sensitive and more caring because of the gift of healings I've received. I continue to pray for God to heal me to be fit to love, strong to suffer, and firm in perseverance.

Heavenly Text

April 30, 1994. + I had a vision of being in my mother's bedroom in Kentucky. I recognized the crucifix over her bed, her furniture. She was very restless tossing about in her bed. Previously, in a phone conversation I had told her about going to see Sister Briege. She had shown no interest and asked nothing about my trip. I was crushed. I believe God was showing me that mother was restless about the unusual circumstances I had been experiencing. She didn't understand and was concerned for me.

May 13, 1994. + Again I repeatedly saw beams radiating from the loving piercing eyes. This repeated vision gives me such peace. It was on this day that I realized this same vision often repeats itself on the 13th of each month. I wondered if it was because of the date, or because Erv and I were going to see Ray Dorian.

Erv and I left for Belleville around 8am. We arrived approximately three hours later and understood we would have a couple of hours before the apparition took place around 1 pm. It was interesting that out of all the cars and people arriving, we immediately ran into Anita, the friend who went with me to Conyers. Neither of us knew the other was coming.

This apparition takes place at a large outdoor altar and amphitheatre, an entirely different setting from Scottsdale (in church) or Conyers (in a field). There were plenty of comfortable chairs to sit in.

Around noon I noticed a crowd forming around a television camera and decided they must be interviewing the visionary. I went to the edge of the circle where I could hear the interview very clearly. I was impressed with the manner and ease with which Ray Dorion was speaking to the reporter. It was surprising to hear him say many of the things that I'd written. A few phrases were almost identical. I thought to myself, "This man has no idea how he is giving me affirmation and courage by his gentle words."

When the interview was over I found myself standing next to Ray's wife, I remarked, "I certainly can tell this is real. Your husband is content with his mission." She answered, "The presence of so many here is the sign to us that God is pleased. Mary brings the crowds." About 4,000 were in attendance that day.

As the crowd dispersed from the interview area, I suddenly found Ray was standing next to me. I shook his hand and told him how pleased I was to be present. I explained we had a few things in common. I told him I was writing a book on apparitions and had also experienced some visions. He immediately said, "Let me give you a hug. It's so good to meet someone else who truly relates. It's hard isn't it? I find others just don't understand. Can we get together sometime and talk?" + God did it again. " Sure, I'd love to," I returned. He took out a pad from his shirt pocket. We exchanged addresses and decided we would get in touch soon. I walked away feeling joyful at the thought God really wanted this apparition to be part of my book. + I didn't even have to ask, Ray had asked me.

All afternoon I kept thinking, "How ironic." I live in the middle of the U.S. I've written about apparitions in the East, in the West, and now the middle of our country. No wonder the cloud shaped like the United States is on my picture with Jesus' face. I'm creating a travelogue for apparitions. Certainly not what I would have ever expected one year ago to the day when I traveled to Conyers.

The afternoon was special, and I sensed the presence of Mary. I witnessed sporadic sparks of light throughout the forty minutes of the apparition. + I prayed that God would continue to guide me. Erv was not as impressed.

When Ray read the message from Mother Mary I felt she was speaking straight to me with the words,"...*all of you need to have courage and be witnesses for each other.*"

May 19, 1994. On this day I spoke with Ray, the visionary, on the phone for about an hour. His genuineness only further confirmed my beliefs of his sincerity. What a comfort to speak with him at length. Over and over, he reaffirmed my thoughts. We spoke of many things. I'll relay but a few.

Ray informed me that he has never read any books or writings on apparitions. He doesn't in order to keep his mind clear and open. He wants to be able to correctly relay the messages that are given to him.

I asked him to explain what happens when Mary appears. He said, "There is an intense bright Light and Mary just steps out of it. She is in three dimension. She is more beautiful than you can imagine."

He informed me that the communication with the Mother Mary was telepathic. She usually answers him before he asks a question. Ray has the gift to remember all that is conveyed to him. He receives messages while the crowd is reciting the rosary. Afterwards he writes the message down to read to those present. He said several people had told him that they see the pen and paper glowing when he is writing the messages.

I assured him the messages were in keeping with all the others from Mother Mary and I'd read many.

I asked him if his wife was envious that she didn't see Mary. He replied, "June has the gift of knowing when Mary is there by smelling roses the entire time. June even announces to me that Mary is arriving before I'm aware of her arrival."

Ray feels the apparitions won't last much longer. He said, "Mary has told me there will be a sign left for the world and all will know that the apparitions were of supernatural origin. No human force will be able to destroy the sign. Many will try but will not succeed."

I found myself feeling an awareness + and remarked, "That's when my book will probably be needed. All those who did not believe or did not go to an apparition site will be curious to find out more about them." He agreed.

Ray also informed me that several years ago he had a near death experience and traveled down a tunnel and visited heaven. His wife told him when she read *Embraced by the Light* the description by Betty Eadie's experience was identical to his.

His statement reaffirmed my belief that God is trying every way possible to let us know death is nothing to fear. We need to believe and trust. We are living in a time of many miracles and supernatural happenings.

It was hard to believe it had been exactly one year since I began this quest. Another circle in my life completed. What a year!

May 21, 1994. + I saw a man with strange looking eyebrows. I wondered who it was. I drew a pencil drawing the next morning to not forget how his brows looked.

May 25, 1994. + I saw the loving eye. Then a long white elongated tube appeared. I saw clouds on either end of this tube. Then an instrument, like a nose-dropper, dropped drops gently into the tube. The vision was reminding me of my hypothalamus vision. I felt the tube was possibly an extension of a body organ. It was definitely something in my body. I wondered if I was receiving a healing or surgery of a blockage of some sort. It also entered my awareness that it might be some kind of an anointing.

May 31,1994. + I had a brief glimpse of a figure of Light. I thought it was Jesus. First a front view, then quickly a side view with additional Light radiating around the entire head structure. I felt tremendous joy.

June 4, 1994. + I was jolted awake by a flash of lightning and a ringing in my ear. I actually felt like I was struck by lightning. I bolted up in bed calling out Erv's name. Exclaiming, "What was that?" I had been awakened other times with a jolt, or a shock, but this was by far the strongest to date and I saw a flash. I was startled to an upright position in bed. I know nature's lightning strikes are an ongoing attempt by the Earth and the atmosphere to reach a perfect electrical balance. Was Spirit sending more grace to help balance me? I felt God was trying to get deeper thoughts into my mind and my heart.

June 6, 1994. + A vision revealed a human face with a piercing eye. I saw and heard what sounded like the hum of an airplane. I thought I heard; *"Now you can get on with your life. You can fly with me. You have accepted my calling."*

June 2I, 1994. + I was awakened with a Light beaming towards me. A dove was flying, in and out, of the Light. The dove kept coming towards me. I decided the Holy Spirit was delivering grace and knowledge.

July 9, 1994. + I saw Jesus carrying the cross over His shoulder. Then I saw Him hanging on the cross. I saw a battlefield, men with guns. I then saw about a dozen individuals huddled together, on their knees. It appeared as if they were being executed. The background, the sky, was very red. My heart was beating rapidly and I was feeling emotions of fear.

July 20, 1994. + Again I saw a very clear large eye with tears running down the side of a nose. This lasted a lengthy time. It felt like tears of sadness.

July 23, 1994. + I started seeing an unusual desert scene. I knew I was inside a spacious tunnel that was made of sand. It was very dark, and I was alone, wandering around inside of it. I felt alone and confused.

Father Mike reminded me, "Your recent visions seem to reflect aloneness. Remember, even Jesus had to go to the desert to pray."

August 18, 1994. + I had a vision of scattered Light coming together to become a picture of Jesus' face. I then saw Him hanging on a cross, His arms outstretched. His arms were higher than His head. I could see His body slumped forward away from the cross. I viewed the scene from above the cross,

73

then a side view, and then several different views of His sorrowful face. I cried and hurt inside. I believe Jesus was asking me to help carry His cross.

August 30, 1994. + I saw an ocean coastline with waves splashing upon the sand. Then the scene zoomed in close and I saw a single set of footprints in the sand. I recalled the poem, Footprints, "*When you see only one set of footprints, know that is when I am carrying you.*"

I felt God was working on my fears. I was trying harder and harder to obey and follow. It was impossible to be content trying to resist His wishes. I knew he wanted me to share more and more.

Sometime in August I received a call from Aunt Martha telling me she read an article in her Kentucky newspaper entitled, "The Miracle of Fatima Continues in a Home." The article was about a woman, named Helen Cleary who lived in Kentucky. She had been healed from crippling arthritis after receiving a statue of Our Lady of Fatima. Helen opens her home to prayer every Tuesday and Thursday to individuals who would like to come to give thanks for her miraculous cure. Martha said, "Why don't we go there when you come to Kentucky. Maybe Helen's story will fit with your apparition stories." It certainly sounded interesting to me and we were already planning a trip to Kentucky in September.

September 13, 1994. Thirteen seem to bring new and exciting experiences, and this one was no exception. This time my mother, Martha, and I went to Helen's just south of Louisville. I had experienced a vision of eyes radiating Light toward me as I had awakened. +

We arrived at Helen's home about 10am. Her home was in a typical neighborhood. We followed a couple of individuals through Helen's backdoor. I instantly knew this was not a typical home. The small kitchen was crowded with an array of Marian literature, rosaries, medals, and pictures, all displayed on the table, counters and sideboards. I smelled fresh brewed coffee and home-baked rolls.

We were greeted with hugs from both Helen and her husband Jay. Helen escorted us into the adjacent small living room. I was struck with awe at the beautiful five foot, wood carved, hand-painted statue of Our Lady of Fatima, which was enclosed in a lighted glass case. The size of the statute in comparison to the room of only about 12x12 was overpowering. The room was tightly arranged with two couches, one on each side of the room, a dozen opened card-table chairs placed in the center, a bench, two other chairs tucked in the corner, and a kneeler. It accommodated about twenty of us.

Mother, Martha, and I took our places in the last row, they in chairs, and I on the bench. The atmosphere fascinated me that the statue created as it towered above us amongst the crowded room of smaller statues, pictures of saints, crucifixes, and multiple family pictures. There was an array of 8x10 family pictures everywhere. There were nine pictures of infants, nine pictures of first communicants, nine pictures of teenagers, and multiple pictures of grandchildren. I felt I was in a home full of love.

The room filled quickly and quietly. Helen entered, turned on a tape recorder, knelt on the kneeler, and a male voice from the tape began to lead the prayers of the rosary. Shortly I began to be filled with a warmth, like I receive at the time of a vision, and I knew that God was at work. I had a ringing in my ear, and without further warning, I saw the spirit image of Mother Mary lift from the statue and float to the corner of the room. The spirit was of color but translucent. This all happened suddenly and lasted only briefly. My tears began to flow as the bird in the cage in the kitchen burst into jubilant song. I felt the presence of God everywhere. As I shook with pleasure and delight I whispered in my heart, + "Thanks God, you have once again surprised me with a gift." I turned to Aunt Martha and asked if she had a handkerchief.

My insides were warm and tingling and my mind whirled

with thoughts. All present prayed three decades of the rosary. Sometime during our prayers, I witnessed another spirit, a nun that seemed to emerge from the side of the room. The spirit floated into a picture of Sister Faustina, which I hadn't previously noticed. + This confirmed for me that the spirit was Sister Faustina. Both sightings had startled me. When the prayers were finished, Helen turned and looked at me, "We have a guest. Nancy, what do you want to tell us?" I was shocked. How did she know what had just happened.

I gave my heart a second to ask God, "What am I supposed to say?" and timidly began. I introduced myself, and my companions. I then heard from within, +"*Tell them. Tell them.*" I reluctantly said, "I'm writing a book on apparitions. That's why I came here." I kept feeling this prompting inside saying, "*Tell them. Tell them.*" I continued with, "I received a gift here today, (I again heard, +"*Tell them. Tell them*"). I saw Mother Mary's spirit lift from her statue and go to the side of the room. I believe God wants me to write about this place."

Helen beamed with glee and jumped up exclaiming, "Oh, I'm going to be written about." She ran into the other room to fetch something. Several individuals reached out with their hands and touched me saying, "It's her." "She's the one." "She's come." I felt disconnected but overjoyed with peace and pleasure. I wondered what was transpiring. I was then informed that Mary had told Helen someone was coming to write about her.

A lady named Bonnie proudly was uttering praises and statements saying, "God has sent you here. I'm working with a new organization with priests and you're going to be our author. Father is receiving messages from Jesus. Jesus told Father He was sending an author. Father told me I'd know when I met the person. You're the person. Jesus is going to be dictating to you messages for priests. Not just a book but volumes."

I'm sure I looked puzzled, but pleased; confused, but elated. Half of me felt like I was dreaming. Everyone was asking me questions. Bonnie was saying, "Write down your phone number. I'll be calling." Some were showing me pictures. Some were asking me to sign the guest book. It was a twirl of emotion and commotion that was mystifying. I was shaking inside and felt as happy as the bird that had been singing earlier.

Shortly, Helen approached handing me a four by four inch little booklet of eight pages that she had typed of her experiences. She placed it in my hands with a reverence saying, "I only finished third grade. I don't spell real good or type good, but it will answer all your questions about me." On the front was written in longhand, **"How it all began. Why I have no answers. I only know it Happyened**." (Helen's title and spelling.)

Helen then encouraged me to look at their picture album. She explained that the statute had been found in the back of a warehouse in Fatima, where it had been for over forty years.

I remember saying to Jay, "How wonderful for you to open your home to share with others." With tears he said, "Yes, it's really hard. I don't know why God picked Helen, but He did. We have a big family and they are all supportive."

I saw my mother sitting, looking bewildered, as Jay shared an album filled with pictures: the statue's arrival and Jay making the case that holds the statue. I was surprised to see pictures of Mary that did not look like the statue. In one of the pictures Mary's hands were raised to her face, instead of being folded in front of her. I could clearly see the wooden statue in front of me and how it was carved. + Jay remarked that different individuals often get unusual pictures. I remarked, "Aunt Martha why didn't you take pictures today? That's your job." She answered, "I guess today I wasn't supposed to. I'll come back and take some for you." Jay gave me a copy of the two pictures with different hand placements.

As I drove home, one can only imagine how stunned I felt. Mother looked very perplexed. She had previously read some of my writings, but had been non-committal. She had viewed the tape from Scottsdale that I had shared on our last visit and had not said much. Now, she said quizzically, "That was really weird, those people saying they knew you were coming."

I kept hearing over and over Bonnie saying, "Jesus will dictate to you. It will be volumes." Was I going to hear an audible voice? I had heard an audible voice that said, "Write." I've been hearing His voice internally for some time as +'s. I didn't know if I'd ever tell anyone what Bonnie had said. Maybe Erv, Father Mike and Jane. I did know, though, that I was supposed to add Helen's story to my writings.

Martha read Helen's story to us as I drove home.

***

Helen wrote...**How it all began**: I came from a large family, the youngest of 10 children with only a third grade education. One of my less endearing and most remembered qualities was that I was a gossip artist. You had no business telling me something, if you wanted it kept a secret.

Through the years, arthritis had turned me into a chronic complainer. I complained about everything until I got my way. People, especially my family, would give in just to shut me up. I lived with this agony and so did others nearby me for 14 long years.

The simple everyday activities walking up and down the steps in my home or even holding a pot of coffee were just too painful. Periodically, I would get cortisone shots, the strongest dosage possible to control the pain.

The arthritis was so bad that for 14 years I could not kneel. My husband and son did the housework and even helped with other chores. For quite some time, Jay wanted to build a ramp by either the front door or the back door to make it easier for me. In pain and frustration, I answered with anger that it didn't really matter.

In my mind, I was making plans for my funeral. I was not going to stay in this world as crippled as I was. Trying as hard as they could, my family could not do anything to please me. My daughter would come in to bathe me and to fashion my hair.

Memories of my two brothers, one sister-in-law and one niece who took their lives appeared to be the course my life would soon follow. I told myself that I would probably go straight to hell, but that's okay because I was living in hell now. Sadly, I realized by no means that this had to be right.

Looking for Mary: March 1992: I read an article about the 75th anniversary of Our Lady's appearance in Fatima, Portugal. Being crippled with arthritis, I still wanted to do something special. While attending the

Heavenly Text

Blue Army meeting, I asked what their plans were for the celebration of this Diamond Jubilee to be conducted later this year?

They indicated they had many plans already under way. I questioned if it would be possible to obtain a statue of our Lady of Fatima for this great event. After much discussion, the Blue Army organizing committee members commissioned me to arrange for the purchase of a statue for the Living Rosary Procession to be held in October at Bellarmine College.

I went to Mass early one morning and prayed for guidance. A thousand questions would soon be answered through the assistance of two ladies, especially one who lived in Portugal. I specified that it must be a five-foot tall statue of Our Lady of Fatima, very beautiful.

Within a few days, I received word that the only five-foot statue that could be found in all of Fatima was one sitting in the back of an old warehouse, and it didn't look very beautiful. There wasn't a demand for hand carved statues and soon a decision had to be made. The lady who lived in Portugal, Dorothy Miller, returned to the warehouse.

Looking into the statue's deep, brown eyes, Dorothy Miller whispered softly, "You are going to America!" The Blue Army arranged for the purchase

Jay (my husband) and I arranged to pick her up at Standford Field (Louisville, Kentucky) on August 15, 1992, the feast day of Mary's Assumption into heaven.

Finding a miracle: During all of the excitement when Jay was carrying the statute of Mary into our home, I ran upstairs to get a piece of glass. The glass alone weighed about seventy-five pounds and was going to be placed on top of the table where the statue would rest.

Suddenly realizing how heavy the glass was and the task of carrying it down the stairs again, I heard a little voice tell me "You can do it."

I was not aware that Jesus had healed me on that day. In about three or four days, the events of this week would reach a climax.

It was on a Friday. Jay left for the country and I was home alone. I was angry with him and my son, Bradley for not doing the laundry. Once again, the little voice told me, "You can do it."

I did go down the steps.

I did do the laundry.

On my way back up the stairs, I heard a little voice ask, "Can I be a guest in your house?"

Sitting in my big overstuffed chair, I laughed at the absurdity of the question. My grandchildren don't even want to see me unless they absolutely have to for some special occasion.

I haven't knelt in 14 years, and you want to be a guest in my house. At that time I really didn't know where that voice came from, but three times it said, "You can kneel."

Taking a moment's pause before the beautiful five- foot, hand carved,

Heavenly Text

painted statue of Our Lady of Fatima, I knelt down. For the first time in 14 years I was able to do this without pain. The feeling of exhilaration was ten times better than winning the lottery.

In all of the excitement, I literally jumped up on the couch and on the chair. But in all of the excitement, I realized no one in my family was there. After the shock of feeling no pain, I cried that I wanted to tell the whole world that Jesus had healed me.

I don't pretend to understand why Jesus had done this for me. I am a chronic complainer and horrible gossip. This I do know, Jesus had taken away all my pain.

When my family returned from the country, I ran out the door to meet them and quickly jumped on a ten-speed bike. My family was shocked. The neighbors were in awe. It has been years since I learned to ride a bicycle, but I had never been on a ten-speed.

On October 1, 1992, feeling like a recycled teenager, I jumped a ditch and broke my leg in three places. Jay was furious with me. He asked, "Woman, what did you go and do now?" A few moments later we arrived at my doctor's office to have the leg checked out and he too chimed in the second chorus of "What have you done now?"

The day following the "Living Rosary Procession," I returned to my doctor. I repeatedly told him I felt fine and that it was healed. Refusing to believe me he ordered another x-ray.

The technician compared the new x-ray with the one that was taken during the initial office visit and just could not accept my story about Jesus healing me. She also could not explain how something like this could have happened. On October 22, a third x-ray was made and confirmed the results of the second x-ray, that there was no evidence that any bone was ever broken!

The doctor's orders were to keep a cast on my leg for 30 days in spite of the x-ray findings. I tried as hard as I could to cut the cast off of my leg but at last I could not. A butcher knife would not phase it.

Remember how I said I like to gossip? Well, now I had a good story to tell. Jesus had healed me and I wanted the whole world to know.

I would tell my story to people at church. I would talk about it at Kroger's, the ballpark, everywhere. Soon people were coming to see the beautiful statue of the Blessed Mother. This did not please Jay. "Woman, when are you going to stop bringing strangers into our house?" he would ask, "I'm not getting any of my work done!"

We later agreed that on Tuesdays, people would come and listen to my story about Jesus' healings and how He gave us His mother from the cross as recorded in John 14: 25-27. When the people come I talk them into praying Mary's beautiful rosary.

Since Mary arrived as a guest in my home on August 15, many people left behind stories of faith. The miracles that have taken place in the lives of so many are more that I can count on my fingers and toes and on Jay's fingers and toes.

***

Later that afternoon I went to meet Erv at the golf course. He was mingling with other golfers. I could hardly contain myself. I wanted to share all my wonderful and exciting news. I waited until we were alone in our car. I relayed everything. We prayed that we would be able to handle whatever it was that God had in mind. That night, I had + a vision of eyes and streams of Light radiating towards me. I believe I was receiving graces, a thank you, for going to Helen's.

As I looked back over my last three visions, I believe God was showing me in the desert, patiently waiting, for the gift of seeing Mary's Spirit.

The next morning before we left for home in Missouri it felt wonderful to hear Mom say, "Nanc, I don't envy you. Yesterday sure was eerie, but I support you. I'm trying to understand. I'm behind you." How long had I been waiting to hear those words? Over a year and a half. She also told Erv she felt sorry for him and how hard it must be.

As we drove the seven-hour trip home, I relived, over and over, every moment of the last few days

The day after coming home from Helen's, I took communion to my friend Jay, the paraplegic who gave me his pin to take to Sister Briege's. When I arrived, the first thing he did was reach over his head to a shelf on the wall and handed me a bottle of holy water from Fatima. I thought, "How does he know I just had a Divine encounter with a statue from Fatima?" He said he had been thinking about showing it to me before I arrived and knew he was supposed to. I shared my story about Helen and seeing the spirit of Mary leave the statue. He was in awe. I was in awe that Mary had me telling the story.

Heavenly Text

The next day, I brought communion to my neighbor, Mary Alice, who was confined to her home. She was diagnosed with cancer a couple of years ago. I've witnessed her good times and her bad times. She has had much suffering in her recent life. She had been in remission of her cancer but was now experiencing a new problem because of a weakened immune system. I wasn't there but a couple of minutes when she said "I just received some holy water from Fatima this week. Maybe it will help me." (Amazing, I'd heard this twice in two days.) I knew Mother Mary wanted me to share the story of Helen with Mary Alice. When I told her, she was very moved with a show of tears and said that hearing my story helped give her strength. I figured with these two occurrences Mother Mary was trying to teach me to speak more openly about my life.

When I returned home from Mary Alice's, I phoned Helen in Kentucky. I shared my two stories and began asking her many questions, so I could write about her. She informed me she was 65 years of age, the mother of nine children and grandmother of nineteen children. She informed me that she heard from a friend of a friend about a lady who lived in Portugal. Her name was Dorothy Miller. Helen called her for assistance and it was Dorothy who located the statue. When I asked Helen to explain her physical condition before her cure she informed me that doctors had advised her to have replacements on all of her joints and limbs. She had refused because it was too exhausting to think of that many surgeries without a guarantee she'd feel better.

When I asked Helen if she ever had visions or got messages she replied, "Mary talks to me often. Ever since she's been in my home. She's always saying, *'Tell your guests. Tell your guests. Tell them. Tell them.'* (I chilled, remembering how I heard, *'Tell them. Tell them.'*) But I have not been telling anyone until recently."

She explained, "I went to confession and I explained to a priest I was getting messages from Mary. He was very stern with me. He shouted at me to the extent my friends outside of the confessional could hear. He said I was just trying to bring attention to myself. For my penance he told me I was forbidden to ever tell anyone Mary's messages. I was confused beyond belief. Here, a priest, who represents Jesus, told me not to tell; and His mother was saying *'Tell them. Tell them."* I suffered a great deal over this and was very upset until I found a confessor who believed me. This priest talked to the bishop, who talked to the other priest, and it finally got worked out. Mary told me she was so sorry I had to go through that terrible pressure and hurt."

Helen says most of the messages from Mary contain statements of prayer, messages of learning to love one another. Once Mother Mary told Helen she had been hard to communicate with and that she had wanted to communicate to her since 1984. This confused Helen until she mentioned this to her parish priest who reminded her that he had made a trip to Portugal in 1984 and had invited her and Jay to go along. They had declined.

Helen and I ended our conversation knowing we would speak at a later date. I told her I'd come visit the next time we came to Kentucky.

The next morning I picked up my Bible. The pages opened to the section on prophets. I cried, shivered, prayed, and asked God for all the grace possible to help me understand and continue His work.

I read Jeremiah, "Ah Lord Yahweh; look, I do not know how to speak: I am a child!' But Yahweh replied, 'Do not say, 'I am a child'. Go now to those to whom I send you and say whatever I command you. Do not be afraid of them, for I am with you to protect you - it is Yahweh who speaks!' Then Yahweh put out his hand and touched my mouth." (Jeremiah 12-9)

I shuddered as I remembered the day before hearing + the ring in my ear, which I now know was God's touch. Thoughts of being God's messenger scared me.

I prayed, "God, can I do this? Do I have the strength?

Heavenly Text

Who and what am I afraid of? Please, God, give me peace by molding me into the person you want me to be. Teach me your way of thinking. Your way of prayer, your way of reaching out to others, your way of speaking to others, your way of following orders, your way of living, your way of suffering, your way of dying. Your way of reaching peace. I long to hear your voice and bring rest to my soul. Open my heart, my ears, and my will. I love you."

Gift of Knowing

As I start this chapter I pray, "God, please shower me with your love and knowledge and give me wisdom, courage, and perseverance as I continue with this book of your messages. God, give me the gift of knowing your will. For to know your depths, I feel I must first know the depths of myself. My soul is like an urn longing to be filled. Open my heart to understand your heart. My reaching out is my response to your love that I feel you are extending to me. Fill my soul with spiritual knowledge. Fill my soul with Divine knowledge. I love you."

Shortly after returning from Kentucky I received a package from Aunt Martha, containing the diary of Sister Faustina, entitled *Divine Mercy in my Soul*. (Sister Faustina was canonized a saint by the Roman Catholic Church in 2002.) I began to read it immediately. My heart and mind could not read fast enough as I learned what Jesus had dictated to her. I related to her words. She spoke of her interior knowing and feelings from Jesus, that I know and call my +'s. I was fascinated by the fact that even a cross (+) was inserted in her writings when she received messages. No wonder I saw her spirit at Helen's. God used us in a similar way.

I certainly identified with Sister Faustina when I read of her visions, and her fear of talking or writing about them. She wrote about the lights she experienced, the flashes of lightning, and the visions. Sister Faustina always realized when the word was from God. She wrote, "The word of God is clear, nothing can stifle it." The warmth she experiences when she is having

Heavenly Text

a vision she referred to as the flame of love, the flame of the Holy Spirit. I decided to adopt her statement. I remembered thinking some time ago when receiving a vision, "What is this, a hot flash? Do visions have something to do with menopause?" I chuckled thinking of the difference in how a nun explains and how I write. I remember Jane saying, "God has a hilarious sense of humor." So deep down I know He approves, no matter how I express His words.

Chills and warmth went through my body as I read message after message she had received. Sister's writings were confirming and affirming my experiences. I was impressed with Sister Faustina's willingness to take on the suffering of other souls. I feel I'm doing well if I can save my own soul. I question how much God expects. What will He expect of me? But then I know He never sends more than one can bear.

In reading Sister Faustina's writings on suffering, I better understand how we're all in this together. As I read, I had an interior knowing, + Jesus permitted me to think of illness as a disorder in the order of the universe. Therefore any suffering restores this order. He started with His Passion. We, His co-creators, also continue to help to restore order by our suffering. The disorders of our physical self (disease, handicaps, illnesses) cause physical suffering. The disorders from anger and hatred cause physical and mental suffering. The disorders from our neglect to our environment cause the earth to suffer. The disorders of our air cause animals, plants, and humans to suffer. The disorders of the feelings in our heart cause anguish instead of joy. Every trial and suffering is helping not only oneself but also all mankind and all of creation. +

However one wants to look at it, we are all participating in the suffering that Jesus went through. For me, this explains justice. I pray He continues to help me to endure whatever His will sends my way. My confirmation on the above thoughts came today when attending Mass. I felt His assurance, + His flame of love, His presence, as the song *Be Not Afraid*, was sung.

The following week, my friend Patsy from Georgia called,

Heavenly Text

"I don't know but this might be a God Message for you. I've been wanting to tell you to read *The Poem of the Man-God*." When I inquired what the book was about she replied, "Jesus dictated to Maria Valtorta the story of His and Mary's lives. It's very lengthy." (Vatorta, 1897-1961 is the author of over 15,000 pages.) I had an interior knowing that I should read these books. God was sending more affirmation my way.

I located the five volumes of *The Poem of the Man-God*. I learned that Jesus also gifted Maria Valtorta with visions. She writes in a very descriptive way.

The major part of the first volume is the life of Jesus, which begins with the birth and childhood of Mary. The other volumes are Jesus' public and private life, His passion and resurrection, and the assumption of Mary into heaven. For me, these writings were another confirmation and affirmation. They read like an extension of the Bible by adding depth to the apostles' stories and Jesus' parables. The culmination of all the books resonates deeply because they are the words of God. He speaks to us all in different ways yet in the same way. He is offering us many opportunities to reach a better understanding of His mysteries.

Jesus says to Valtorta, "*It is nothing to remember the words of the gospel if its spirit is not understood.*" Jesus explains to Valtorta the spirit of the word more clearly. He explains how mankind needs to evolve more spiritually in order to become holier, and how the world will receive salvation through Mary. I was elated when I read, *"There will be many returns among the children of man, whom I love notwithstanding that they are weak. And I will fortify them; I will say to them, 'Rise! I will say: 'Come out! I will say: 'Follow Me', I will say: 'Listen', I will say 'Write' and you are among them."*

"**Write**." + I know I heard a voice say the word, "**Write**." Another affirmation. There is no way to explain how I chilled and my insides quivered. I thought, "You're right Patsy, I know I was definitely suppose to read these."

Reading the volume on His Passion brought even a deeper

realization that Jesus wants us to better understand sorrow. Sorrow comes to all ages and in many forms: grief, loneliness, misunderstanding, pain, hurt, frustration, and jealousy. We have to understand charity to understand sorrow, to understand justice. Jesus explained that the worst of His sorrow was the anticipation of His passion. He explained how the sorrow of knowing the future was greater than the physical sorrow both for Him and for His Mother, Mary. He explained that it is a gift from God to not know what is in store for one's life. I agree. If we knew the future, half of us would never get up in the mornings. He explained that His sorrow still goes on and on. The repeated message is that we are all in this together with Jesus to conquer pain, sorrow and suffering. The key is **All Together**. + Sin is nothing more than trying to figure out what to do right. We must all learn from others' sins in order to alleviate sin.

Jesus explains to Valtorta: *"Sorrow is not a punishment, when one knows how to accept it and use it rightly. Sorrow is like priesthood. A priesthood open to everybody. A priesthood that confers great power on the heart of God....*

When I read this message I wondered if my writings were for this type of priesthood, not ordained priests but all people. Doesn't it say in the Bible we are all priests of Melchezeidek?

I know we need to learn to speak of God and to God. Prayer is speaking to God. When we pray we grow closer to Him and then it is easier to speak of God who is present in us and in everything. As time goes on we are supposed to be learning to grow into charity by listening and learning. We have been hardened by the ages. If we learn to be humble and obedient and to grow in faith, we are learning the orders that come from on high, from God.

Jesus explained God does not just give. We have to work at and improve ourselves through His grace to become holier. God works at our hearts. When our hearts are weak, we suffer inside; as our hearts grow stronger we suffer with, and for, others and ourselves. But one's heart has to be open in order for God to speak to it. Jesus says, "*When a soul lives in charity, its heart is calm and it can hear and understand the voice of God."*

God doesn't speak to an agitated heart. One must be open. I have learned one has to have humility, obedience, and faith, and then comes wisdom and knowledge. I've come to understand that we are born with limited knowledge and our inner desires grow because we want perfect knowledge. God abides in our hearts when we learn true love, love of neighbor as ourselves. God is found in charity. I believe when one finds charity, God finds us. There is no painful search. He finds us. And when one has God, he/she is successful in all enterprises. Then we become teachers for each other, generation to generation.

I pray: "Please, please, make me strong. Help me to understand your wisdom. Keep me humble. Help me to understand and carry your words to others. Help me to be able to enjoy this joy you're giving me without being proud. Help me to be able to speak to those you wish and not to those who do harm. Give me the strength I'll need in times of strife and turmoil. Please God be there for me as I am here for you."

Then a book arrived from Jane, called *The Way to Divine Love* by Josefa Menendez. Immediately, I discovered it was another book of Jesus' dictation. I thought to myself, "Why haven't I ever heard of any of these books of dictation before now? + The arrival on my desk, one after another, was uncanny.

Sister Josefa endured trials that seemed foreign to me. She exemplified an outstanding life. She personified "Thy Will Be Done." I was somewhat confused but impressed with her life. Jesus spoke of her weakness in doubting his dictation's and visions, but also at her strength of will to endure suffering. He confides in her that she was chosen to suffer to help other souls obtain heaven. Again, that same powerful message. It was comforting to read a lengthy dictation where Jesus explained suffering.

Jesus explained the deepest of love is in sharing sorrow. I

know I have a long way to go to totally understand this mystery. I have learned through my life's experiences that in order to understand pain we have to become involved with pain. We have to learn to bear others' pain and sorrow in order to learn. Sharing in others' sorrow is what teaches us what pain and suffering is about. As we take on other people's pain we grow spiritually. I have come to understand that the more pain we take on the more joy we begin to feel. This, to me, is a large part of the mystery. It's what Jesus was teaching through His passion. Jesus could have ended suffering but He chose not to. Suffering is part of life with Jesus. If we suffer with and through Him we are helping mankind. Once we learn to overcome suffering we will have mastered the mystery that is the core of Christianity.

We are a society obsessed with healthy life-styles. We are a death-denying society. In denying death we deny immortality. To accept death is a conscious decision to accept life. It's the reason we were born. The same goes for suffering. We are a pain-denying society. By joining our sufferings we are reaffirming life. I believe suffering is necessary to bring the mind and body into submission to God's will. One is either the slave or the master of his sufferings. Sufferings can make one free. Jesus suffered to conquer. By continually uniting our sufferings with His we are all helping in conquering evil. The fact that Jesus knew the past and the future He knew others would be joining with Him in suffering to redeem the human race. It's by uniting our will with His will that this comes about. When we unite ourselves this way we become one with Him.

I think after these three books I better understood. I like to think Jesus is saying to me, "Help me remake the world." I now relate to the quote on sufferings in Romans 5:5.

Thoughts on suffering continued to prompt more thoughts on pain and healings. Some people just see God in the good whereas I now see God in the good and the bad. I see the whole picture as His plan for us to recognize our immortal self, the self that does not die -- our soul. Pain in life, physical or other, teaches us to become full human beings, and is part of God's plan to bring us to His level of thought.

Illness is a natural part of life just as death is a natural part of life. Nature heals itself instinctively, so I ask, "Can man learn to heal himself?" I'm beginning to think so.

I think back to Pam's statement, "God talked to me last night. He told me this was all for a purpose. Not just for me, not just for our family but also for many people. If He can suffer and die on the cross then certainly I can do this."

I now know and realize the huge implication of her statement. Jesus shared His insight with her in a way that she understood. Healing is a personal matter for each individual. It is a matter of growth, of development, in learning to let go and put everything in God's hands. Healing is when we touch the deepest core of ourselves.

September 17, 1994. I experienced an amazing vision. + I saw a bright outline, glowing with Light, that I knew was Jesus. He was placing His hands on the head of a person kneeling. I knew that person was me. I was overwhelmed. I was witnessing what appeared to be a ceremony. Then I saw a set of footprints going up a set of stairs. I knew in my heart Jesus was carrying me, one step at a time.

The feelings I felt were very powerful. I knew I was receiving a special blessing. Jesus laid hands on individuals to heal them. Was I receiving a healing I didn't understand?

Later that morning when I went to read my Bible I became somewhat frustrated with all the pieces of paper I had in various places for markings. I have the habit of placing a piece of paper when a scripture verse deeply resonates. + Periodically, I remove these markers and record them for further references. I thought to myself, "Markers are building up. I haven't recorded Bible readings for some time. Some of these have been here for a long time. Today is the day to clean up the marker mess."

As I pulled the markers out, starting at the front of the

Bible, I began to read. I was utterly amazed at the sequence of the verses as I removed them. It quickly became apparent, and felt eerie, when I realized this procedure had a purpose. +

(Numbers 12:6) Yahweh said "Listen to my words: If any man among you is a prophet, I make myself known to him in a vision. I speak to him in a dream." +
I had marked this when I hadn't told anyone of my visions. I had never typed that verse before, feeling the message was too bold to even consider applying it to myself. I knew the verse explained what was happening to me, but I couldn't admit it to myself.

(Duet. 34: 9) "Joshua, son of Nun was filled with the spirit of wisdom, for Moses had laid his hands on him." +
My vision from earlier that morning, of Jesus laying His hands on my head, immediately came to mind. I was overwhelmed and began to get warm all over. I became immersed in heat, the flame of His love.

I prayed, "God, I can hardly believe it, but I guess I've known for some time. I think you have bestowed upon me the job of being a so-called prophet, a messenger in writing for you. I'm deeply moved and honored. I'm fearful and frightened but willing to submit myself to you. I'm scared and uncomfortable to admit to anyone that I might be what one would call a prophet. Now I feel you are telling me to accept my calling. Continue to be with me, as I need to know you are here with me at all times. I'm scared. Are you sure you want me? I'm so weak and not worthy. I love you."

Then I nearly fainted when the next marker I pulled was from (Psalms 61:1) +

> God, hear my cry for help,
> Listen to my prayer!
> From the end of the earth I call to you,
> With sinking heart.
> To the rock too high for me!
> Lead me!

Heavenly Text

For you are my refuge,
A strong tower against the enemy.
Let me stay in your tent forever,
Taking refuge in your wings.

I had a hard time believing this verse followed the prayer I had just written down. Obviously this one from Psalms is better, but similar.

(Eccles. 6: 14-1)"A faithful friend is a sure shelter, whoever finds one has found a rare treasure. A faithful friend is something beyond price; there is no measuring his worth. A faithful friend is the elixir of life, and those who fear the Lord will find one. Whoever fears the Lord makes true friends, for as a man is, so is his friend." +

I thought of Jane. It was her birthday. I made a mental note to call her later. She wasn't in her office but I left a birthday wish with that scripture message.

(Eccles. 14: 20-23) "Happy the man who meditates on wisdom, and reasons with good sense, who studies in his heart, and ponders her secrets." +

What have I been doing? I know I'm happier in my heart than I've ever been in my entire life. I think I'm beginning to know and understand God's ways. +

(Hebrews 12:29) "For God is a consuming fire." +

I often feel this fire, the "flame of love" when I experience a vision. I'd been feeling this all morning.

(1 Peter 6-9) "Through your faith, God's power will guard you until the salvation which has been revealed at the end of time. This is a cause of great joy for you, even though you may for a short time have to bear being plagued by all sorts of trials; so that, when Jesus Christ is revealed, your faith will have been tested and proved like gold-only it is more precious than gold, which is corruptible even though it bears testing by fire-and then you will have praise and glory and honor." +

These verses today all fit together too much to be a coincidence. + Definitely a huge God message here. Thanks God. I'm speechless. I heard interiorly, + "Nancy, admit it to

93

yourself. You are a prophet, a writing prophet."

No one will ever know how hard those words, *"You are a prophet, a writing prophe*t," were for me to type that day. It took every ounce of strength and courage I had to admit that God had chosen me for a job. No wonder I'd saved all those pieces of paper and hadn't written them down. I didn't feel I was worthy. I still don't.

I asked myself, what is a prophet? I looked up the definition in my Bible: A prophet is one who has an immediate experience of God; he is one to whom the holiness and will of God have been revealed; he contemplates present and future through the eyes of God; he is sent to remind men of their duty to God and to bring them back to obedience and love.

(This definition certainly helped answer my questions about seeing past and future events.)

I thought, "Doesn't God want us all to reach an understanding of his will and become one with Him? Isn't that the ultimate quest?" I know being a prophet is a goal God wishes all of us to reach, and each one of us can if we take the time and listen to His voice in our heart.

September 18, 1994. + In a vision I saw lots of Light circling around my head. The Light kept entering and exiting my ear. This lasted for a long time. The experience ended with a dove flying away. The experience was very powerful and peaceful.

I believe I was being shown that my visions are Jesus' dictation to me. I recalled, "The Holy Spirit, whom the Father will send in my name, will teach you everything and remind you of all I have said to you." (John 14:26) I felt this vision was an affirmation for my writings from the day before.

As I continued to wrestle with understanding visions, I discovered an interesting article in which scientists spoke of visions as altered states of consciousness. I learned that over a quarter century ago, an institute founded by Robert Monroe had patented an auditory guidance technology based on the natural functioning of the brain. This is called the Hemi-Sync Process. Researchers were using the science of sound to explore altered states of consciousness, which they called dissociative and transcendent states. When volunteers attended this institute and participated in the research they saw visions and heard voices in the process. Studies showed that people who used this process could control pain, strengthen the immune system, hasten recuperation from surgery, lower blood pressure, and enhance recovery of speech and motor skills after a stroke.

It was good to read that some scientists were actually trying to prove these phenomena. Scientists in the past have always studied what they could observe directly and investigate experimentally. Now it appeared some were studying consciousnesses.

I felt they were trying to explain our soul. Pre-historic men rose from various depths of knowledge. Is it time again? Science and technology are going faster and faster. I believe we are trying to catch up with God's thoughts. I wonder if God isn't letting mankind experience the supernatural in varying ways to find answers about Himself and science so we can become one. I wondered if in time science would discover and prove the soul is the mind. I wondered if this would interfere with our belief systems of religion.

I rejoiced reading this quote from Willis Harman, M.D., past president of Noetic Science. "I can imagine a science based on the assumption that we contact reality in two ways: First is through physical sense data, which forms the basis of normal science. Second is through a deep "inner knowing" an intuitive, aesthetic, spiritual noetic and mystical sense."

I continued to gather information. I learned that the Light that Buddhists experience in meditation is called the knowingness and oneness realized, a natural and commonplace spiritual experience. They refer to the Light as the energies of

95

the mind or Kundalini. They work at meditation in order to reach this enlightenment. I understood that individuals pray; meditate for years, to achieve this enlightenment, or Kundalini. If that's what I was experiencing I knew it came about naturally, without any attempts from me. My visions were a gift from God. Then I read that some individuals reach Kundalini without even believing in God. This really confused me. But I read over and over that when one reaches this realization about God everything opens up for them. My first explanation of God Messages.

I read more about chakras, and how they are the invisible energies of the body associated with Kundalini and have a complex interaction with the neurological and the physiological systems in humans and appear to be the interface between Spirit and man. I also discovered from the consensus of various religious cultures, that science and scientists, do not know how to explain this phenomena of chakras and Kundalini. The belief among many yogis is that there is need for further scientific study in order to reach an understanding of the peace and happiness that is associated with Kundalini. My readings suggested that the awakening of Kundalini, the light experienced, is integrating states of consciousness into a great, more harmonious mode of living. The Kundalini was also described as the dynamic power in us. I read that some thought this dynamic power and spiritual knowledge worked together, hand in hand, and that the perfect harmony of universal consciousness began in the conscious evolution of the human soul until it reached the transcendental self. It was thought by others that when people experienced Kundalini they could incorporate it into their lives, giving them special powers, such as healing and mysticism.

I read and learned that in India, yoga was common practice. Yoga's aim of meditation was to open the unused potential of the human brain, called Kundalini. Investigation of Kundalini in India is to know and learn the intelligent forces of creation. In ancient books in India the flow of energy, this unidentified force of creation, is called prana. Prana is another name for energy. Accomplished Yogis talk often about discernment of different levels of this energy: an extreme case being mystics or geniuses, the other-extreme mental disorders. The enlightened ones are those who know how to balance this energy as part of their self-discovery: a genuine person who tries to unite the vital power and spiritual knowledge with the evolving spirit of life. I liked this definition, as it seemed to resonate with my Christian beliefs. I reasoned that possibly the Christian mystics down through the years have known and experienced Kundalini, but did not have the free expression that we now enjoy to explain what was happening to them. I wondered if the Holy Spirit was the Christian term that matches the word Kundalini.

The more I read, the more enlightened and more confused I became. I accepted the fact that copious amounts of information kept coming to me, and I knew I was to write about the information. I "did not" know how I was going to apply all of it to my life. I "did" know that there is much more to life than the reality I see and touch.

Mystical occurrences seem unusual, but I'm convinced many more individuals experience supernatural happenings than we know about. Individuals avoid public comment out of fear. I often wonder if my mystical experiences are due to the circumstances I've been exposed to, my personal pursuits, my personal response, God's choice or all of the above. I question where and when does our choice stop and God's start. The supernatural has a way of making me feel elated and ecstatic one moment, questioning and doubting the next. I feel in step, then out of step.

September 23, 1994. + I saw lots of movement of Light, but I couldn't clearly distinguish what I was seeing. I felt like I was out in space viewing from above. I saw a human hand holding what looked like a small world. Why was God telling me He was holding the world in His hands? Why was it so small? Was He telling me that the world is just a small part of the universe?

October 3, 1994. + It was a very short and quick vision. + Jesus appeared to be standing by my bedroom window. I jumped to a sitting position and looked across the room. I saw nothing. As I closed my eyes I saw a cross fading away in the distance.

I presumed Jesus was letting me know He was always with me, and that I would be sharing in His sufferings.

October 8, 1994. + A vision of a view of the world. I first thought I was looking at a globe, and then I realized I was looking down on the world. The scene moved to the California coastline. The scene changed and I saw the southern tip of the state of Florida pull away, out into the ocean. I saw other places but couldn't clearly distinguish what I was viewing. I wondered if I was viewing future happenings? I remembered the vision of the hand holding the world.

October 11, 1994. + A vision in which I felt I was drifting into outer space. I suddenly saw a very clear door in the sky. Then the scene faded away. I wondered if this could be the door to heaven. I recalled + "Behold I stand at the door and knock. If anyone hears my voice and opens the door, I will enter his house and dine with him, and he with me." (Rev.3-20) I had a powerful understanding that Jesus was knocking at my door. The door I saw in this vision had no handles on the outside. His message seemed to be saying to me *"the door can only be opened from within."*

October 13, 1994. + I was awakened with a vision seeing the eye. It was very clear and very large, with big streams of Light streaming from it towards me. Then a tear ran out of the corner of the eye. I saw a hand holding the world in its palm. I remembered seeing the smaller version of the world in the palm of a hand in an earlier vision. I felt the warmth, His flame of love. I realized it was the 13th. I had plans to go see Ray Dorian that day.

I had previously let some friends know I was going to Our Lady of Snows again. I let it be known that anyone could go along. We'd meet and car pool. Privately, I asked God to send only those He thought would be supportive of my thoughts and my writings.

When I woke up and discovered it was a rainy day I thought to myself, "Why are you doing this, and in the rain again? You know Mary is here with you. She's everywhere." But I had individuals counting on me. I'd heard interest in going from twelve women. So I got up and went to meet them. Only seven women showed. We decided to go together in one person's van. We left in the rain to travel the 140 miles.

When we arrived the rain was only a drizzle, and by the time of the apparition the rain had stopped. My Aunt Martha drove up from Kentucky. She brought my cousin and another friend and we found each other easily. There was a crowd of about 5,000. While the rosary and other prayers were said, Ray visited with Mary.

Afterwards, he delivered Mary's message. The rain had started up again, but it was very light. I recalled the horrible heavy rain that had begun in Conyers after the prayers and thanked God I didn't have to sit through another storm. Ray also gave us sad news. He told us his wife June was suffering from throat cancer and he asked for prayers for her. He informed us that Mary had said she would not return until February 11. Mary would not be coming to the shrine on the thirteenth as she had on the previous thirteen monthly visits.

While Ray was speaking an unusual occurrence took place. A white dove appeared and flew to the top of the shrine. The dove perched on top of the shrine and looked out over the crowd for the entire time Ray spoke. Ray talked for about thirty minutes, delivering Mary's message and his personal messages. It was mesmerizing to watch the dove. I have no doubt the entire crowd was processing thoughts of the Holy

Spirit. When Ray finished speaking, the dove flew into the crowd landing on one lady's head, and on to another person's shoulder. For a time the bird walked along the ground amongst the crowd and I saw several children stroke it. All of this was extremely moving. I kept wondering if someone had brought a tamed dove. But then I questioned how could someone train a dove to go to the top of the shrine and sit for thirty minutes. Don't birds take shelter in the rain? I've since learned that white doves are not unusual in Missouri, so possibly, one lone dove just felt the prayerful energy and decided to join us. Or?

What warmed my heart the most was our trip home. One of the woman suggested we start a prayer group. I was thrilled. I'd desperately been feeling the need for support from others. I also yearned for feeling God's presence among friends in prayer. I knew joining with other souls in prayer would add depth to my soul. We decided we would attend Thursday evening Mass at the Newman Center and meet afterwards to pray for forty-five minutes. We would start within two weeks. I silently thanked God for answering my request.

I'm convinced uniting prayer with others adds to the accomplishments of prayer. This uniting of spirits grows into much strength. I feel until prayer flows out of us and into the world it's not really accomplishing much. Jesus taught us how to pray by speaking to His Father in Heaven. The Our Father is a universal prayer for many.

Over and over, I have read that Jesus and Mary say pray, pray, pray. Prayer is the tool by which God works within us. God wants us to live a prayer-filled existence. I think God expects us to continue to grow in prayer daily, which in turn makes our love for him grow. Prayer is a never-ending search for closer union with God. All prayer is an act of faith that reconnects us to God's presence. God expects us to pray not only in petitions for wants and desires but also in thanksgiving and joy.

There are many kinds of prayer. **Prayers of petition** are what most people think of when they think of prayer. It's normal to ask for gifts and blessings. Prayer comes quickly in times of terror or sadness. Many of these kinds of prayers are answered if we have a close relationship with God, a strong belief system, and a reverence with gratitude and thanksgiving.

There are many **formulated prayers**. Jesus gave us the Our Father as a special prayer. Many prayers may be formal and repetitious. One of these is the prayer of the rosary. I think the rosary is Mary's way of teaching us to meditate on the mysteries of the life of Christ. The rosary reveals Christ's character to us. The rosary's purpose is to open the door to our minds and hearts to a waiting friendship and relationship with Christ. The rosary can be a starting base of conversation.

Seeking knowledge of God is prayer. One can do this by listening to God's word when reading the Bible. There are many spiritual and secular books that can enlighten us in the understanding of God's ways.

Silent personal prayer, uniting our minds with God is another level of prayer. This is called contemplative prayer or meditation. This form of prayer does not always come easy. We have to work at it. We need to pray not just with our body, but also with our mind, our imagination, and our hearts. We can ignite a prayer that resonates with our whole being, and this prayer helps bring us into union with God. Then God can gently ease us into change, when and where it is necessary.

There is **community prayer**. For Catholics this could be the Mass. There are many various ways people join together in prayer in many different religions and customs around the world.

Charity is the purest form of prayer. Charity, (love) needs to be sincere and from the heart. God tells us many times that what we do for others is the ultimate that He seeks. Through charity with others, family, friends or strangers, we grow in love. If our charity is without concern for thanks or for profit for one oneself, we accomplish whatever our hearts desire. (Phil 4:4-8)

I know that in some mysterious way when we pray and

feel one with God, our will joins His will. Putting prayer in God's hands is, "Thy will be done." Spirit absorbs our prayers and takes over. Miracles begin to happen.

We desperately need prayer for our world that is in such turmoil. We see unrest, anger, war, and negativity manifesting everywhere. Mankind has lost its sense of responsibility. God didn't create unrest; mankind does by turning away from God. Acting and living as a spiritual person is hard because we live in a world that does not readily recognize spirituality. But I believe we are born with an innate desire to do what God wants. Children are born innocent. We need to find that innocence again as adults. We need to approach life with reverence and imagination. Co-operation among all of us is a necessity in order to find world tranquility. Jesus needs us to help bring about His Kingdom here on earth. I think this will come through prayer, courage, and trust. We can all do it together.

Often I've asked myself, "Why all of the apparitions on the 13th?" Then one day in prayer an answer came. + *"Christ is the vine and we're the branches. We are all connected. Praying together makes the power of prayer stronger. If more believe and are praying in unison, more could be accomplished. A larger belief system would be at work. Since the 13th is the day Mary has picked it would be beneficial for all to pray in unison at that time. Make it a prayer for peace. Inner peace. Not a lull between wars but an inner peace that is necessary for union with God. Each person's contribution of love from the heart is to help bring about His Kingdom. Souls at peace united with God would radiate love, joy and peace uniting this troubled world."*

October 19, 1994. + I was awakened to a vision of seeing the Light of an individual, standing alone. I knew it to be Jesus. The left half of His body was covered with white clouds. The exposed right arm raised and gave me the blessing sign. I felt overwhelmed by the power of the gesture. I thought maybe it was a thank you for writing about prayer.

Heavenly Text

October 27, 1994. A vision in black and white. I could see only shadows of people. + I observed many hands folded in prayer. I then saw a dove fly over the praying individuals. This was very profound to see because that evening was to be the first meeting of my newly formed prayer group.

When our group met we bonded and I felt a peace. The evening had a mystical feel about it. I did not tell the group of my morning vision, or of any of my visions for that matter. I knew God was answering my prayers for a support group, but I just wasn't strong enough or ready to tell them what I'd been experiencing. Would they believe me? Would they laugh at me? How would I go about it? I promised God I would tell them soon, but not yet.

October 30, 1994. + A vision of the piercing eye. Then I realized I was viewing the world again from up above. I saw the outline of Jerusalem and felt danger. I then saw an island; I thought it to be Haiti. Then I saw another place but I couldn't tell where it was. It was an unfamiliar body of water. I again saw the tip of the state of Florida pull away into the ocean.

Within days I read in the paper of a terrible accident in Jerusalem. A train wreck had caused an explosion, and fire was carried throughout the streets on top of floodwaters. Much devastation and injury resulted. Shortly thereafter, I read that Haiti had terrible rain and mudslides, with over five hundred dead. Then I read where Florida experienced the hurricane named Gordon, with many tornadoes, high winds, destruction and deaths. Knowing of these disasters in advance and seeing them occur made me feel helpless. I questioned why God showed me these in advance. I believe He was asking me to pray.

November 1, 1994. + This vision reminded me of my vision of the embrace. I saw the parting of clouds while viewing the piercing eye. There was a feeling of increased intensity as the clouds repeatedly opened and shut, over and over again. I wondered if I was again going to feel His

103

embrace. My insides heightened in awareness, with feelings of eagerness. Then I saw an unusual geometric design radiating towards me. It looked and reminded me of a symbol a cartoon artist might draw of radio waves. I immediately prayed, "Am I going to hear your voice? Now? Am I going to see your face? What is happening?" The radio wave signal repeated itself several times. Then the vision and the eye faded.

I was confused. Did this mean my communications with God, my visions, are the only voice I will hear speaking to me? Will I hear an audible voice? Are my visions the voice? Is this vision telling me more strongly: "This is me?" Was I not open enough? Could I have heard a voice if I were more open? Will these visions continue longer or was this like broadcasting an "Over and Out" symbol. Was this going to be the end of my visions? I questioned and questioned.

When I talked with Father Mike, he asked if I had ever reviewed the sequence of my visions, to see if there was a pattern to them. He also suggested I reread all of the prophets in the Bible.

I began to read the words of the ancient prophets, to try to better understand visions. I read, over and over, where God told the prophets, "Tell others what I tell you." In my heart I knew I wasn't following orders by not revealing mine. Each prophet I read seemed to be giving me a message, "*Write yours down, write yours down.*" I had been keeping a personal log of my visions but had not typed them into my writings. The prophet's words felt like an assignment. I began typing them into my manuscript, which you are reading.

Jesus the master of the all the prophets said, "And therefore what the Father has told me is what I speak to you." (John 12:50)

I started reading the book *God, Dreams, and Visions.* Thank you Morton Kelsey for giving me added confidence. I wrote him and thanked him for helping me. He responded with a personal letter. What a kind man.

Heavenly Text

November 25, 1994. I experienced the presence of two intense-loving eyes. + One came closer and closer until I thought it would invade my face. Then I witnessed tears coming out of the corner of the eye. I realized Jesus was letting me know that He appreciated me typing my visions into my writings. I believe the tears were tears of joy.

November 26, 1994. On this day I finished typing all of my visions into my manuscript. (Since I had dated everything it was easy to go back and insert them.) I wrote: I now <u>know</u> that receiving these visions for the past year and a half have changed my life. I <u>know</u> I am no longer the same person. I <u>know</u> I've grown. Feeling and experiencing God in this profound way is almost indescribable, but I'm trying my best. It's what I think God wants. Visions are not something I could or would have ever dreamed up. I question why God has chosen to share them with me. I feel honored. I know I'd miss feeling His communications if they stopped.

I better understood how God was teaching and guiding me. The progression of the visions made more sense as I typed them. Each vision seemed to flow with the events I had been writing about. I finally understood how visions were giving credence to my writings. Typing all of them gave me more comfort and peace as I began to <u>know</u> and understand. I realized how God was working with me in a laid-out plan. I felt His guidance + as I typed and processed their deeper meaning. I realized I should always study visions in groupings, because the messages become clearer and more meaningful.

God must have approved because that night I encountered a night of phenomenal, almost inexplainable, spiritual, mystical occurrences. I received a thank you. + As the vision began I knew I was experiencing a unique happening as I began to feel a profound awareness of God's power and presence. I thought the movement of Lights and shadows that I was witnessing were Jesus and Mother Mary. I saw beautiful eyes amongst the movements and began experiencing an overwhelming sensation that I had never felt before. I chilled, not a short chill of excitement, but my whole body vibrated all over and I shook with chills for several minutes. To explain the sensation is almost impossible. It felt like an intense pull, an uplifting, a vibration, and a yearning of utter bliss. I prayed in thanksgiving and wonderment as the sensation swept over me. I was reminded of the word tremble in Psalms. Over and over I chilled, and my body vibrated with the amazing divine feelings, which seemed to last longer each time as it repeated itself, time and time again. Once during the extraordinary powerful moments I heard an audible rattling noise in my ears and my body felt very unusual. It was that ear thing again. The voice of God? At times I wondered if my body was trying to lift higher -- to levitate. All of these unusual mystical phenomena seemed to go on for a long time. I was well aware that I was awake but definitely in the control of a higher power. I remember praying and talking to the presence and actually hearing answers to my questions. Mostly I made statements like, "Jesus I know this has to be from you. Mary is that you? God, why am I being showered with these feelings? Thank you for your Divine presence. Help me to remember this beautiful moment. I love you."

I felt I was being treated special and reveled in every moment. My encounter was a magnificent spellbinding experience from the Divine. There was no mistaking who it was from. I knew from the depths of my soul. I think God really was letting me know He expected me to write down the visions. He was thanking me. He wanted me to know that visions are His voice, His communications. I felt His loving presence as He raised my consciousness to one with Him in mutual knowledge and love. I can say without a doubt, when the moment comes that God makes Himself known to all mankind, everyone will know, without a doubt that they are experiencing a supernatural occurrence. Whether one accepts this realization in their mind or not will be up to each individual's faith and belief in a higher power.

In time I went to sleep. When I awakened I relived the experience in my mind. My mind was whirling with excitement and I decided to rush to my computer to relate the happenings even before telling Erv. I wanted to give God the praise and glory He deserved for this Divine encounter. He had showered me with a wonderful gift. + I know He can manifest Himself in a way that leaves no doubt when one receives. I know this gift He gave me is available to all.

I now know + without a doubt that I'm the designated writer. I feel my mission in life is to share, to write, to spread the word to those who are not having these experiences, as well as to reinforce those who are. I still question. Am I open enough to do what He wants of me? Where is He leading me? What does He expect me to do next?

I remembered reading several times in the messages of Jesus and Mary, that a time was coming when every man and women on earth would know God exists. I think the knowing of God will be comforting to many, startling to many, terrifying to many, and even ignored by many. But I know, without a doubt, they will know when it is from Him.

I still often seem to jump mentally in and out of two thought patterns. I am learning more day by day. Just as Moses fulfilled his destiny, I'm working on mine, by listening and responding to God's call. It's back to "Thy will be done." I have come to know and put God as the center of my life. I know true acceptance of His call consists in becoming like a child. This submission of surrendering myself unconditionally to God is not easy but requires real strength and courage. Those who follow this path know of what I speak. I also know I'm not perfect and I have a long way to go, but at least I take comfort in knowing I'm on my way. God's pull is strong, the feelings are deep, and I know the call is from God.

I started meeting Jesus, like a spark, when I began studying His written word in scripture. For me, His word has become more and more powerful. Accepting His words in scripture meant acknowledging the power of His words. I know the force of His word is His voice. The word of God became real when I started putting His words into practice. The words in Scripture are what have sustained His instructions throughout generations. For me, accepting Jesus' words meant accepting a new way of thinking.

Now, I <u>know</u> and understand Jesus' words with a deeper faith. I <u>know</u> I have begun to experience the Holy Spirit in a new profound way. I feel I've been taught divine knowledge and spiritual knowledge through God messages and visions. Through His guidance I'm learning the peace that comes from being aware of His presence. The peace that comes from doing for others. The peace that comes from attending daily Mass. The peace of seeing His presence in all of nature and all of existence. The peace that comes from being one in thought. The peace of mind that allows love to abound. The force of Jesus and the work of the Spirit in my heart make me <u>know</u>. I just <u>know</u> that I <u>know</u>.

The next morning my Bible mysteriously opened to Timothy. I shuddered when I read, "Make use of your time until I arrive by reading to the people, preaching and teaching. You have a spiritual gift which was given to you when the prophets spoke and the body of the elders laid their hands on you; do not let it lie unused. Think hard about all this, and put it into practice, and everyone will be able to see how you are advancing. Take great care about what you teach; always do this, and in this way you will save both yourself and those who listen." (Tim 4:13-16)

I pray, "Thank you God for an unforgettable experience of love that you bestowed upon me last night. Please teach me to be humble as you shower me with these gifts. Thank you for the gift of your Spirit. Daily teach me and mold me that I will not embarrass you but make you proud. As I realize today begins Advent I know + it was no accident that you filled my night with wonderment to share in your writings at this time. Help me to share with others throughout this Advent season the magnificent joys you bestow upon me. Thank you from the depths of my heart. Enhance my knowledge, Lord, and help me to overcome any and all kinds of disbelief or unsettling that tries to enter my awareness. I love you. I give myself once again to you to be led by your Truth and Light."

When I finished rereading this chapter I was astounded how many times I had typed the word <u>know</u>. I decided to underline each. I discovered God was really letting me <u>know</u> that I now <u>know</u>.

Gift of the Spirit

Jesus says, "I tell you most solemnly, unless a man is born from above, he cannot see the kingdom of God. I tell you most solemnly, unless a man is born through water and the Spirit, he cannot enter the kingdom of God: what is born of the flesh is flesh; what is born of the **Spirit is Spirit**." (John 3:3-6)

Mankind has, in a sense, forgotten how to exist. We, as a whole, have lost the imagination and the mystery that is the core of faith. Many equate faith with religion. I believe it is much more than that.

For me, faith is a belief system that guides a person's behavior and gives purpose and meaning to life. Knowing, believing, trusting in God is the added dimension that gives significance for the reason for life. Faith means the mind trusts God, the heart responds to the love of God, and the will submits to the commands of God.

Faith is being touched by the Holy Spirit. Faith is given when we are open and willing to accept it. When touched by the Holy Spirit, we come to know God in another realm. This gift is available for each human being.

When one has faith then one can seek the peace of God. Most think this peace is obtained only from dying and going to heaven. I have come to believe that one can reach some of this peace here on earth. I have come to believe death is as easy as life - like pregnancy is easier than birth. It is imperative that we learn from life and search for this peace here on earth.

Peace comes from facing responsibility - not fleeing from it. To feel peaceful by being preoccupied with oneself, to withdraw from today's trials and tribulations, to withdraw from the responsibility of sharing the burden is to fail to the purpose of what it means to be human. Peace comes from involvement, not detachment. We all are not privileged but each of us can serve a great purpose.

Faith can be and should be the connecting point for all religious cultures and belief systems. God made us all, He watches over us all. The method one uses really does not matter. All humans have different spiritual rituals, practices, and prayers. It's in the quiet and stillness of the mind and heart that He talks to each of us. God shows no partiality. He wishes all to be saved. He offers His call, His grace to everyone. The Holy Spirit is what can unite us all.

We read in scripture that Jesus' life was filled with the Spirit. Jesus was conceived by the power of the Spirit. He was baptized and anointed by the power of the Spirit. The Spirit drove him into the dessert. He cast out demons by the power of Spirit. He healed and performed miracles in the power of the Spirit. He rose from the dead to give us a share in this same Spirit. Jesus needs and expects us to continue the work He began here on earth.

We are all one family rooted in God, destined for heaven, in various stages of falling back and getting up and trying again. It takes work, hard work on one's spiritual life, and lots of prayer to attain His goals. But I've come to the realization it is what He expects from each of us.

I pray that God continues to teach me to expand. I know the more the Spirit enters my soul the more I seek God. I know it is necessary to put all into God's hands. Poverty of spirit is necessary for genuine growth. Poverty of spirit is the willingness to trust God for transformation. It's never ending. This is the mystery I now deal with. There is no end. I know the meaning of the words, "Blessed are the poor in spirit." My tiny spirit and His Infinite Spirit - together we go forward. As St. Ignatius says, "I came from God, I belong to God, and I am destined for God."

When the Spirit helps, lifts me up, holds me in His arms, He is accepting and loving all my experiences and me. My faith continues to come together and is falling into place like the pieces of a puzzle. The fascination is never ending. I feel the Holy Spirit has been carving me like a stone to become one with Him.

I continue to write, all for the glory of God.

November 27,1994. + I saw two piercing eyes with tears running out. I was questioning if the tears were of joy or sadness when I heard the phone ringing. The nursing home was calling to inform me they were taking my friend Bill to the emergency room because he was choking. Bill had recently asked me to be his power of attorney, so they had to notify me.

I witnessed a sigh of relief from Bill when I arrived at the hospital. I immediately was able to help with communications. I could tell the doctor was really upsetting Bill because he kept talking to the nurse or myself and not to him. I informed the doctor Bill was very intelligent. I asked him to please direct his questions to Bill, because Bill was the patient. I tried to explain that just because Bill had noticeable multiple physical problems did not mean he didn't understand.

I was glad I was there to help. As we passed time just sitting in the emergency room between doctors' visits and tests, I thought a lot about my Pam and all she had gone through. I was thinking how alone Bill is in this world. I kept remembering the tears in the vision earlier in the day. Was God telling me I was sharing in His sufferings? In my eyes Bill has suffered daily since the day he was born. I knew in a small way I was assisting and helping Bill to carry his cross. I knew Bill was also teaching me more about how Jesus wanted us to treat others.

After four hours of tests, frustration, and three doctors, they decided Bill had the flu, and the mucus from his sinus congestion was causing him to choke. I know I could have come up with that diagnosis hours earlier, but the diagnosis certainly made Bill feel better.

December 5, 1994. + I witnessed lots of Light. The Light

eventually went together and formed a huge circle. It reminded me of the sun. Then the Light seemed to move forward towards me and back again. It got large, then small. This repeated itself several times.

I felt the vision was explaining, "*I'm trying to get closer to you. Will you let me?*"

December 7, 1994. + Again I saw the piercing loving eyes with tears running out. It was the second time for a suffering scene this week. I felt God was bestowing His love upon me, but I felt discomfort. What was I supposed to be doing?

I definitely had mental suffering throughout the day. I believe God was preparing me in the early morning vision, letting me know there are many kinds of sorrow. I felt God nudging me all day. + He was telling me to share my insecurities. I felt His prompting to talk about my visions to my prayer group. I had written about them. It was time to talk about them. All of them. I felt He wanted me to share with the group the knowledge that I was a writing prophet. God strongly was saying to me throughout the day, + "*Give your gifts away.*"

The more I thought about sharing these private gifts the more afraid I became. I discovered that I had to be strong to be weak. Since I'm an accomplished person I know that I project security. I had been feeling somewhat dishonest with my prayer group because they witness my security and not my feelings of inadequacy. I promised God I would tell them everything that evening if all seven of us were present.

Then about mid-day I received a phone call from one member saying she was not going to be able to attend. I felt relief. I wasn't going to have to share my deepest self. That evening I attended Mass. I looked up and the one who had called was walking in late. I shook inside. I had a deep inner knowing. + God was sending me a strong nudge that this was indeed the right night. I knew I was going to have to do what I had promised earlier in the day.

I began our prayer meeting with the prayer I had typed at

the end of typing in my visions. I explained my fears. It was very hard to get the words to come out of my mouth. I began to shake and cry. I trembled as I shared. It was extremely hard to admit to them that I thought I might be a prophet. I finally was able to let go and release my pent up feelings. I fell to my knees. My six friends united in prayer around me. My fear dropped away like the lifting off of armor. The support, the tears, the hugs, the prayers, all flowed openly that evening. I found renewed courage from their prayers. Afterwards I experienced a newness and freshness of Spirit. ("Thanks, God.")

That evening I had a very unusual dream. It was a dream, not a vision. I wrote it down when I woke up. In my dream I felt very strong and I proceeded to turn over three large square concrete stones. The stones felt light as I moved them but they looked extremely heavy. As I turned them over each had writing on the underneath. I could see and read clearly: **I Am the Way. I Am the Truth. I Am the Life**. Immediately, while still in my dream, I was with a friend and I told her about this unusual dream. I explained to her how I had turned over special stones. I told her I realized I was having a spiritual dream. I told her I knew the stones represented Christ. When I awakened from sleep I remembered my dream. I had a dream in a dream. It was a first for me. I realized it was December 8, Mary's feast day. I considered the dream a thank you straight from Christ.

The next morning I decided to write more on prophets. When I began words flowed from within: + *"A prophet is one who is a providential instrument of God for the guidance of His people. God is sending an abundance of prophets today to prepare the way for His next coming. The Kingdom of God is meant to be a community of prophets uniting and standing together. Being a prophet means becoming a disciple of Christ. A disciple is a spiritually mature individual who reads God's word, reflects on His word, then does something that expresses this faith.*"

I was trying to accept the responsibility for making personal decisions on how to live out Jesus' teachings on a daily basis. I was trying to witness for Christ in all that I said, wrote, and did by listening to the voice of His Spirit in my heart. I know God is all and wants nothing more than for **all of us to become prophets** and witnesses to His truth. With this in mind I no longer feel uncomfortable saying I am a prophet. Mind you, I'm not ready to wear a sign on my chest, but I'm feeling more peace.

December 13, 1994. + This vision was extra bright vivid color. I saw part of a face that I knew to be Jesus. I saw the nose, both eyes, and forehead. No mouth. The scene came and left maybe fifteen times. Once or twice I saw blood run out of the forehead and I knew I was seeing the scars from the crown of thorns. Another suffering scene. I questioned if it was to be myself or someone else.

That morning an individual I knew from church had the hospital call to see if I could bring communion to her. I found it no coincidence that about a week before she had asked me if she could read the book I had written about my daughter Pam. After reading *Gift of Life* she asked if I had written anything else. I shared some of my other writings with her. Later she came to my home to return my manuscript and informed me she had been to Medjugorje. She had encountered some profound experiences while there.

Now, she had a malignant tumor on her lung and needed immediate surgery. Did she know the week before? The same surgeon who had operated on Pam's lung was going to operate on her. I think she thought my presence would help. I told her our prayer group and many others in our parish were praying for her. During surgery the doctor discovered the tumor had not metastasized. The surgeon did not order chemo or radiation. He felt he had removed all of the cancer.

I think I gave her comfort throughout the week as I took communion to her after daily Mass. I witnessed her suffering

Heavenly Text

and prayed with her and encouraged her to unite her sufferings with Jesus to make our world a better place for all. I felt I was helping another person share in carrying His cross.

December 14 1994. + While seeing a vision of Light, I experienced a strong spiritual pull. The power was intense. I witnessed lots of motion of Light and figures of people moving about. I saw what appeared to be a group of people praying. I wondered who the group was. I didn't think it was my prayer group. There were too many people. I saw the group part and make room for me. Who was moving over for me? Why? Then I suddenly wondered if I was going to die? Was someone in heaven making room? I kept thinking of Christmas.

When visiting with Father Mike I shared with him that I felt something was going to happen to me at Christmas. I told him how the frequency and intensity of my visions were picking up, and I was feeling this compelling urgency.

We discussed my latest vision. Mike said that when I told him, his first thought was, "Maybe Nancy is going to die." I remarked, "I thought of that too. But I also think He could be asking me to die more to self." He agreed. I said, "Whatever God has in mind is fine with me. I'm ready. I'm not scared. I've told God I'm more than ready for His everlasting peace. I'm curious and wonder what the future holds? How will Erv and the children handle it if I leave?"

I went on explaining, "I definitely think it's easier for the one leaving than the spouse remaining. I've been through death and have always said that I think losing a spouse would be the worst because it changes one's entire life. When you lose a child there's plenty of grief, but the pattern of one's life doesn't change."

When Mike and I finished talking, I asked him for absolution. I wanted my soul to be ready if I was going to die, or if I was going to experience Jesus in another profound fashion. As I shut my eyes and Father Mike prayed with me, I had an amazing feeling of being emptied from head to toe. It

116

felt like a wave passed through me as I viewed the piercing eye. It was another new experience of awe. This occurrence only added to my knowing that God was preparing me for something special.

When I left Mike's company I recalled the many times I've read where Jesus says to those he dictates to, "Your spiritual director is like me talking to you. Listen to what He says." This is how I have always viewed my discussions with Mike. I took his comment on possible death very seriously. I wondered if God was forewarning me so I would be able to give my loved ones a special good-bye. All evening and late into the night I pondered on the thought, "What if I die on Christmas? My poor family. I knew I was probably having many of the thoughts and feelings my Pam encountered. I wasn't scared. I was at peace, but curious. I wondered if I should say anything to my family about my instincts. In my mind I was preparing to leave this body if that was what was in store.

I knew I'd be hurt if Erv knew he was going to die and didn't share with me. I kept thinking I'd probably tell him Christmas Eve. Maybe I'd tell all of the family after the grandchildren had gone to bed. As I stewed and thought, I prayed. "God, please lead me. I trust you. Let it be done according to thy will."

I kept asking for God's guidance. In my heart I felt the need and urge to write a personal letter to each of my family. But I was having a hard time finding the time with just a few days before Christmas with so much to do.

That evening I had a dinner party that had been planned for some time for some of my elderly friends. I have this dinner every year for older widow friends. I call it Grandmothers' night. Our guests were six women, two in their late seventies, one in her eighties, and one in her nineties. I always enjoy cooking for and entertaining them. So often I think we the public forget our senior citizens. Erv always plays chauffeur and picks them up. I love having them and thrive in their company. I never fail to laugh, learn something, and feel good that I might be making them a little happier. It was a successful evening.

Later, as I was in bed falling asleep, I tried to imagine what it would be like to go home to heaven.

December 15, 1994. + I awoke about 4am and again began thinking about how I would say my good-byes in letters to each of my family members. Suddenly, I received a very unusual vision. I repeatedly chilled as a vision repeated itself maybe 30 times. The scene appeared to be a pair of hands, that opened and light would come and go from the hands. This picture repeated itself in many different angles and movements. I didn't understand until attending Mass the next day. While praying it suddenly came to me. + I suddenly realized the hands belonged to me. He wanted me to use my hands more. We had talked at our prayer group about inviting individuals and laying hands on them.

December 18, 1994. + I saw a figure of Light walking towards me. I knew it to be Jesus although the figure was all Light. At first, I wondered if I was going to see Jesus in human form. Then the scene faded away.

December 19, 1994. + I saw a figure of Light. I knew it was Jesus. It came closer than before. The features of the face appeared to be hidden behind a cloud. I felt an intense mystical experience was going to happen. The intensity kept increasing. Then it faded.

December 20, 1994. + I saw the clouds in a vision part, and high in the sky I saw a tiny sun. Then the sun lowered and got bigger. Then the sun rose high in the sky again and got smaller. The scene reminded me of what I saw and experienced at Conyers in May of 1993. I felt Mary was letting me know she was close at hand.

December 21, 1994. + Another bright figure of Light

appeared that I knew to be Jesus. The figure stood up from sitting on a rock and advanced forward making the blessing sign as He walked. I had a strong feeling inside that something major was getting ready to happen. I had seen this figure of Light four nights in a row.

As I lay in bed, I prayed, asking for God's guidance. In my heart, I knew and again felt the need and urge to write a personal letter to each of my family. But when? I lay in bed and prayed and tried to imagine what it would be like to go home to heaven.

(It seems strange to me now to remember how strongly I felt back then that I was going to die. I can still remember how very intense that time was for me.)

December 22, 1994. + I awoke about 4am and again began thinking how I would word my good-byes in letters to each family member. Suddenly I received a very unusual vision.

I was witnessing a toy airplane flying around in the sky. I knew it was a toy because of its square wooden shape. It kept going faster and faster, around and around, up and down. I wondered what this scene was telling me.

Then all of a sudden the toy plane flew into a mailbox. My first thought was, "I am going to die and He wants me to write the letters and to add them to these writings." Then I started wondering, "Does God want me to explain that I'm not afraid to die?"

Then another vision began and the plane was off and flying again. This time I felt like I was the plane and someone was following me very close behind. Suddenly, I went higher and higher and almost out of sight. I thought God was telling me I was going to heaven.

Then another vision started and the plane was flying around and around and started falling downward.

As I lay and thought about all three of these visions I suddenly realized Jesus was telling me, + "*This is another game we're playing. I am testing you to see if you are afraid to die. You are sharing yourself completely by your writings.*

119

You are writing for me. You are sharing your thoughts with your family as you share them with me. You are dying to yourself. These gifts you are sharing by writing are also gifts for your family."

I thought to myself, "How true. How many people write hundreds of pages before they die to explain their relationship with God? And isn't that what life is all about? Learning to know God better."

I received the affirmation of my thoughts with flashes of warmth that assured me my assumptions were right. His flame of Love. Three times it passed over me. The repeated flashes were very strong and left no doubt whom they were from. I prayed and promised I'd continue writing. I was ready for whatever He had in mind.

That evening I went to Mass and on to prayer group. Our group had previously planned to have a Christmas party after our prayer meeting. We met at my home. Husbands were invited; it was the first time some of them had met. After dinner we women sat in the living room and talked, the husbands watched basketball in the other room. I shared with the group my recent thoughts on dying. I told them about the vision I'd had in the morning. None of them had realized I had been processing thoughts of death for weeks.

December 23, 1994. When I woke up about 4am another vision began. + I saw a coffin with someone in it. I questioned if it was me. The vision faded away and then began again. It repeated itself and was clearer but I could not distinguish who was in the coffin. There was a bright light bouncing around like I often see in my visions, a light that I knew to be me. I immediately remembered the vision I had back in early 1994 of a coffin with a baptism gown and host. At that time Father Mike and I had decided that vision represented death to my old self and the start of a new and more spiritual life with God. I felt this vision was again telling me the same thing. The vision repeated itself several times. Deep inside I was still wondering if it might mean a physical death.

Heavenly Text

I prayed, "God, I'm not sure what you are telling me. I know it is a change for my life. Is it physical or spiritual? Whatever, I'm yours. I trust you. Lead the way. Unto you I commend my spirit."

(As I look back now I realize how young I was in my growth. At that time I had many fears. And, obviously, I was still questioning the meaning and interpretation of my visions.)

Returning from noon Mass, I shared with Erv my recent feelings of possibly dying. I told him I thought my morning vision meant another dying to self. But what if I was wrong? What if the coffin meant physical death? I wanted him to know how much I loved him and to know my last wishes. I cried some saying a good-bye from my heart just in case. I then felt at peace inside.

I realized after talking to Erv that death would be my final gift to him, my children, and the world because life is a gift. I have come full circle to the complete realization of the meaning of the title of my first book, *The Gift of Life*. I am not afraid to die. I know my writings are my destiny. I'm doing God's work. If and when I die my life's work will only be continuing the circle of life, because His written word will go on. Life to me has been my God-given opportunity to become who I am. I felt I had accomplished my destiny by following +'s. I now knew true joy, happiness, and inner peace came from giving of myself to others. I love God and I know He loves me. What more could I ask for. My destiny was to be with God here, or in heaven. I was a witness to God's love. My death would be nothing more than going home. I decided I was not going to say anything to my children, who were arriving later that afternoon.

December 24, 1994. I awoke at about 5am and I hadn't slept much because I had come down with a terrible head cold and stuffy nose the evening before. As I was saying and praying a sleepy good morning to God I had a quick vision. + I felt an electrical shock go through my entire body. I saw a man. It was the human form of a man. I knew immediately it was Jesus. It was a man with long hair, clothed in a long robe. He gestured with His right hand towards His left shoulder. I thought, "Are you telling me here's my shoulder to rest on?" Then I saw His hand lift and go directly to where one's heart would be and I saw an exposed Heart. I was stunned, shocked, and thought this must be Jesus' Sacred Heart that I've heard about all my life. I couldn't believe it. An exposed Heart. The vision faded quickly. I spent some time thinking about this mystifying experience. It was as if Christ took birth in my heart - a genuine Advent occurrence. As I pondered on the happenings I fell back to sleep.

When I woke again about 7am my thoughts about the vision were of wonder and delight. The vision had certainly surprised me because I had never thought of Jesus in this way. What had I expected? Certainly not this. I'd often seen pictures depicting Jesus' Heart exposed but I always thought that was the portrayal of the artist. I never really thought Jesus would actually appear this way. I now knew Jesus wanted me to think of Him with His Sacred Heart exposed. I wondered why? (It would be seven years later before I knew the true meaning of this experience.)

I thought about the vision throughout the day. It was a hectic day with a baby in the house and me not feeling up to par. My energy was sapped. We exchanged Christmas gifts in the evening, which was extra special watching the joy and enthusiasm of the two young grandchildren. I was more than ready for bed once the commotion died down around 10pm. My head and body hurt. I knew I had the flu. I hoped the grandchildren wouldn't catch it from me. Their mothers assured me that their families had already had it.

I spent another night tossing and turning, stuffed up, and feeling miserable. Not much sleep.

December 25, 1994. + Up and off to Mass at 8:30am When we returned home, Deanna and family left to have Christmas with Jeff's family in St. Louis. Erv and I cleaned the house of Christmas celebration and I made a quick trip over to the nursing home to see Bill. I knew I wouldn't give him the flu because I thought I had probably caught it from him the week before in the emergency room. I opened his few gifts that he had received from his only niece who lives in Michigan, plus candy and goodies from me. I stayed only a short while feeding him treats. I left for home. I'm sure he could tell I was beat.

I returned home to rest and to try to shake the flu bug. Repeatedly throughout the day, I kept apologizing to Jesus if I had not been as enthusiastic as I should have been about His appearance the morning before. I knew Jesus understood how tired, sick, and disconnected I felt with this flu germ. As I tried to go to sleep I pleaded, "Please give me another peek of you and your Sacred Heart so I can thank you properly. I love you."

December 26, 1994. + Finally, I slept. I still sounded terrible, but felt better. While saying my morning prayers and reading the Bible I thanked Jesus again for the previous vision on the 24th. I questioned Him about the vision of His Exposed Heart. What was I to think? How was I to react? Then I kept having an inner prompting + telling me to again read *The Apostolate of Holy Motherhood*, which is a book of visions and messages from Mary and Jesus to Mariamante. As I scanned the book I realized I had read Jesus and Mary's messages to the author, but for some reason I had not read the visions, which were listed in small print. I searched through the front index and found a section on the "Sacred Heart as My Resting Place." I thought, "I bet this visionary has seen His Exposed Sacred Heart." I rapidly turned to that page.

I chilled, shuddered, cried and thanked God as I read Jesus' verbal comments to the visionary when she experienced a vision of His Exposed Heart. I personally didn't hear His voice or verbal explanation like she did, but I certainly knew He was now saying the same to me. The words resonated throughout my entire body." +

Heavenly Text

"Be at peace. My child. I know this is a great trial for you, but it is necessary for you to be fully united to Me. There is much work to do and I wish to make use of you as an instrument of My Mother's cause. This will require complete filial trust and undying love for Me.

"My Sacred Heart is your resting place and the dwelling of your refreshment. Cling to Me ever so closely as I call your soul to an espoused union of love. Be at peace and rejoice! Do not fear the heights! They are where I dwell and where you must dwell if you are to remain in constant union with Me. The rocky cliff upon which you have climbed is the way to Me. Do not be frightened or discouraged by the steepness of the climb. Be at peace with your struggle. If you but make the effort, I will reach out My hand and grasp you, drawing you closely to Me where you will find rest and the joy which surpasses earthly pleasures. How shallow they are in comparison to the joy, which My love brings to My espoused souls. Blissful and eternal love is yours for the asking, but first you must desire this above all else in your life and proceed in courage and faith in your ascent to Me.

"My Mother has shown you the way. She has prepared My brides for this union of love, to sing praises to God. Hold fast to Me! Cling to nothing or no one else. Call upon My Mother's protection, but think of Me always as your beloved bridegroom.

"The Bridegroom calls His brides to Him; come and dwell with Me. Make my heart your abode. Stay with Me in love; never leave Me. Think of Me always and I will dwell within you perpetually. I in thee and you in Me and together you will dwell in the Trinity, as the Father has promised Me. Be at peace, you have come home. Amen."

I prayed, "Thanks God, you have done it again. You are definitely letting me know I have died to you spiritually. I feel like I'm home. I'm at a loss for words."

That year Erv was lucky to able to take early retirement. He was 55 years old. He had successfully sold commercial insurance for twenty-five years. Prior to that he was a grocery store manager for several years. Erv is a type A personality and I knew it wouldn't take long for him to venture into something new. He soon discovered he loved working for Habitat for Humanity. So in the mornings he generously donated his time to build houses and in the afternoon he played golf. With the winter months upon us, Erv wanted to go south. I wasn't sure if I wanted to leave home. I'm very happy here and don't always understand why retired people want to get away for the winter. I love my home and my surroundings. I love snow and the fireplace. And I wondered whether my visions would continue if I left home.

January 7, 1995. + I had a vision of the eye with the tear.

January 8, 1995. + In a vision I saw the top half of Jesus' face--the forehead was bleeding. Then I saw hands bleeding. I saw multiple sets of eyes with tears. These scenes repeated themselves many times. I knew Jesus was sending me messages about his sufferings, but I wasn't sure why.

January 13, 1995. The feel of someone tugging on me awakened me. I looked at the clock- 2:45am. + I shut my eyes and saw Mother Mary and Jesus. The feelings were powerful.
Later at Mass that day I saw the living eye over the bread and chalice at the time of consecration.

January 14, 1995. + I saw a vision of clouds parting, and then large circles of Light, like the sun. Then a very clear huge eye appeared. I felt the stare of the eye looking into mine. The feeling was overwhelming and powerful. I felt I could melt.
Erv and I were in the midst of a discussion about vacation when the phone rang. It was our friend Andrea. She and her husband go to Gulf Shores, Alabama, each winter. I had met Andrea the week before and she told me about a young woman she had met in Gulf Shores whom she thought I might be interested in meeting. The young woman, Anne, had helped

relieve troublesome foot pain for Andrea. Andrea had said, "When Anne was working on my feet, all I could think of was you and your foot problems. I told her, "I must tell Nancy about you when I get home. Maybe you can help her feet."

Andrea just happened to call while we were discussing vacation. (+?) Andrea said, "I'm in the middle of cooking dinner, but you've been on my mind, and I wanted to call and give you a Realtor's name in Gulf Shores and Anne's phone number." She continued, "Call the Realtor in Gulf Shores and tell him you want to scope the place out. He'll show you around. He'll probably even take Erv to play golf. I think you'll like it there. If you don't like it you can move on to another place along the Gulf."

I commented to Erv, "That's the second person today who told me they thought we'd like Gulf Shores." My friend Judy, a prayer group member, told me she had met an interesting woman, Judy D. when vacationing in Gulf Shores who practiced sound therapy. My friend commented, "I kept thinking of you when I met her. She talks and thinks like you do. I know you should meet her. You two would have so much in common." (+?)

I called Anne (her name is changed to protect her privacy) that evening and introduced myself, and asked if we could meet, sometime, somewhere. I said, "I'd be happy to come to you." She informed me she was going to be at Gulf Shores again in a few weeks. I was beginning to think a vacation in Gulf Shores was a "meant to be." + After further discussion, Erv and I decided to give the Gulf a try. I called the Realtor the next morning.

Here in Missouri, the week before we left, we had an unusual amount of snow, 19 inches, so I got to enjoy the winter scenery. The night before we left I had an unusual vision.

January 25, 1995. + I was awakened by a powerful electrical jolt. I jumped and hollered out a surprised cry that even awakened Erv. I saw the loving eye shedding tears. I saw the Florida coastline and thought maybe an earthquake was to take place. This vision repeated itself several times. Then after a time I saw a lock, chains, things that made no sense to me. I saw an unusual hook and chain, which didn't make sense. I wondered what God was trying to convey to me.

When we got to Gulf Shores we met with the Realtor and found a house to rent for a month. We settled into our rented house on the beach. I was glad to be present to view God's power in the ocean. Waves to me feel like God's Spirit rolling into my body.

Anne called and made an appointment. I was looking forward to meeting her.

The first night in our new location I was awakened with a vision that repeated the vision of January 25, that I had before I left home.

January 27, 1995. + I again saw a hook and chain. This time the scene was clearer and lasted longer. I realized the hook was trying to connect to a chain. Then several times I saw a hook connect to a chain. The hook appeared to be in the middle of a lengthy chain. Suddenly it dawned on me that God was telling me this vacation was involved in the chain of events in my life. My interest heightened in anticipation of the month ahead. I knew I was in God's hands again and prepared for more of His education. I thought to myself, "I've had education for my mind and soul, I guess it's time for education for my body."

January 30, 1995. + I was wakened by another strong electrical jolt. I had a vision of the loving eye and then all of a sudden I saw a large face of an Indian with tears running down his cheeks. I didn't know what it meant. When I met Anne later that day and learned she had studied in India I understood.

Anne came to our place on the beach. We discussed and talked about her profession for a long time before she began working on my body. I learned she had been involved in healing work for over twenty years. When I heard her background I knew I was in good hands. She has a master's degree in physics, and a degree in psychology. She lived in India for two years studying Ayurveda medicine. When she returned to the states she became a homeopathic doctor, a massage therapist, and earned masters degrees in six types of holistic medicine.

I knew immediately that Anne was a gift from God. She explained she would give me a massage and also use reflexology and acupressure. She said, "We have little rivers of invisible energy in our bodies. Through pressure I can help activate these energies which then become beneficial in healing." She asked if I knew of these energies. She spoke of the psychic and spiritual centers, chakras, which exist within us. I explained I had read about this energy, had had acupuncture, and I felt all energy was of God, from God, and connected us to God. She agreed, and explained how she is trained in many ways to help an individual get in touch with the energies of their body in order to help heal and prevent disease. She explained that by manipulation and pressure she would be able to restore active energy in my feet to alleviate numbness and restore flexibility. She explained that nerve impulses need stimulation to allow the natural cellular force of the body to recuperate itself.

She explained further that body tissue, especially connective tissue, has memory. When an injuring force occurs, the tissue that receives the force is changed. Some times tissue retains this energy. The human body either dissipates this localized impacted energy and walls it off, or increases kinetic activity to return it to a normal state. When it is walled off, the body adapts and the human energy field is forced to move around this area instead of through it. This is when clinical problems develop. The use of hands can help the body realign and correct this problem in many ways. We are accustomed to relieve pain with medicine and medical procedures instead of getting rid of the original problem (be it emotional, psychological, etc.) that caused the pain in the first place.

We said a prayer and then she began. Immediately, I felt our hearts and minds unite, and certainly our spirits, and I knew deep inside God was going to heal me more through her loving hands.

Our first visit was fruitful. After examining my foot Anne said it was an unusual problem that she'd never before encountered. She administered strong pressure. It was painful, more than I thought it would be, but I could feel her love and concern. In a little over an hour she was able to activate and renew some energies in my foot, break up some scar tissue, and I began to get some movement and motion that I hadn't felt in years. She cautioned me to soak my feet in order to relieve soreness. "The ocean is the best, the salt works wonders. Bury your feet in the sand. The sand has healing properties," she urged enthusiastically as she departed. She beamed and was thrilled with her success. I heard her joyfully exclaim in a low voice to herself as she left bouncing down the steps, "I can hardly stay in my skin. I get so excited when I help someone that I feel I could explode!"

January 31, 1995. + During the night I saw an abundance of Light. Lots of Light. Lots of colors. Many configurations. Anne had worked on me that afternoon and I think God was letting me know that His Light was definitely being activated in my physical body.

My foot was very sore and I soaked in the tub several times the next couple of days. My foot was still sore when she returned several days later. Again, she was able to apply tremendous pressure and succeeded in getting my foot moving even better. Upon finishing her treatment she insisted that we walk down to the ocean. She buried my foot in sand next to the ocean and let the salt water seep into her "hand-made cast." When I got up to walk thirty minutes later I was amazed at how much soreness the sand had removed. She remarked with glee, "I know why people love to come to the beach. They receive energies from God not only through the sun, but also through the ocean water, and the sand. The healing powers in all of them are wonderful." I had to agree. I was mad at myself for not following her directions earlier.

In four weeks time, Anne worked on my foot five times. Each time I felt improvement. Each time we chatted away and learned more about each other. I knew she understood "God messages" when she commented, "When I was a child, about twelve, I read a book and deep within I knew that my calling in life was to work with people, with my hands, helping them to heal their bodies." Anne frequently travels across the United States, living and sharing God's Spirit as she helps and teaches others. I was lucky enough to be in her path.

We discussed and exchanged thoughts on life energy, and spiritual energy, and how both work in our lives. We discussed electricity and how it has been around forever, how it took men thousands of years to discover it, harness it, and put it to work, although it was always there. Now men were beginning to learn how to harness mankind's internal energies to help in healing. We discussed the essence of God, God's supernatural spiritual energy, and how all energies are connected. We agreed that when the natural comes in to contact with the supernatural something has to give. She said, "When one's energies are balanced and one totally surrenders to the Spirit, healings occur."

Needless to say, I loved our conversations. I'd found another soul mate, another mind that resonated with mine. I thanked God for bringing us together, I thanked Anne over and over and for being a vessel that God could use to restore newness to my foot. For me, Anne represented a person continuing Jesus' work. She is love, she is joy, and she is peace. She's God's hand working for Him. ("Thanks, God.")

February 9, 1995. + I was awakened by a very strong electrical jolt. No vision. It was the day I had planned to meet Judy D.

It was another adventure. I went to visit Judy and learned about her work, healing with sound. I was skeptical at first, to say the least; but was amazed after Judy recorded and charted my speech sounds. She then was able to explain how she perceived my physical problems with my foot. She explained she located the sound I was missing. She made a tape of these missing sounds and had me lie on the couch and relax. I thought to myself, "This is weird, I bet it doesn't do anything." Within seconds I was proven wrong. I had a strong electrical shock go down my left leg and foot. I was dumbfounded. I jumped, let out a shriek, and was forced to believe what she said was true. I knew her treatment was going to complement the work Anne was doing.

How do sound and health work together? Judy tells me she works part time at a clinic in Michigan and their work is called healing with life sounds; Bio-Acoustics. She said, each cell has the capacity of replacing distressed frequencies which provides the body with means to repair itself when damaged from internal and external forces that cause deficient electronic energy. Bio-Acoustics is the body of knowledge dedicated to understanding the meaning of specific, individual frequency or series of frequencies thought to emanate from living systems. These individual frequencies, known as signature sounds, are a combination of genetic coding, geographic local, brain, and neural functions, bio-chemistry, emotions, physical structure and environmental influences. It is documented that the human body is made up of electronic vibrations, within each atom and element of the body, each organ and organism having electronic vibrations necessary for the sustenance and equilibrium in the organism.

Judy D. explained that she could make a cassette tape of my missing sound wave and if I played it while I was sleeping or working in my home it would help restore the missing energy wave I needed to repair my foot. Judy told me of many successful documented cases including herself. She had been cured of arthritis by listening to her missing sound waves. ("Thanks, God, for bringing Judy into my life. Her knowledge and work is again your hands in action.")

Anne and Judy's professions were both intriguing. I was

thrilled to be a part of what I think will be part of the medicine of the future. I had read about alternative therapies and now I was a part of two kinds of them. God was teaching and helping me to understand the healing energies our bodies have had since the beginning of time.

Many times I have talked about the energies of God surrounding us- - the energies of the universe and His energies of love. God was teaching me how to use my own electrical energies for my physical betterment. These two procedures help bridge a gap between medical practices and subtle energy medicine. Neither cure disease but help abate the area long enough for the body to cure itself. I'm sure some people are more knowledgeable and effective in administering these procedures in accordance with their training, and I'd been exposed to the best.

February 10, 1995. + I was awakened by a strong electrical jolt. I saw Mother Mary. Then I was witnessing a priest saying Mass, elevating the host, and then another robed person came up behind the priest and stabbed the priest in the side? What in the world is this about? Was it a future or past happening, or a symbolism for me? I wondered if my writings were going to be a pain in the side for priests?

February 12, 1995. + A vision opened and I could see the coastline of the Gulf of Mexico. I saw the state of Florida and the scene moved up the west coast to the gulf where we were staying. I remembered my earlier vision of seeing the coastline of Florida. The scene was very clear. At first it scared me. I wondered if God was trying to tell me something bad was going to happen. Then there was lots of light around the area and I knew the vision was confirming God's presence. I knew the earthquake was going to be in me. "Thank You God for the on-going physical healing of my feet. I know you played the main part + in training Anne and Judy D. and arranging for me to meet them. Words can't express my thanks for the noticeable recovery of my foot, although I've expected a

132

healing since the day you whispered in my ear at Conyers, +
*'Not much longer.' Thank you for your love and your trust in
my love."*
I was to meet with Anne again that afternoon.

February 16, 1995. + I was awakened with a strong
electrifying jolt. Stronger than usual. I even heard a sizzle. I
felt movement. Erv said I hollered out, "Earthquake." As I
tried to restore calm to my body I wondered if it meant my life
was again getting ready to go through another growth, another
change. I felt God was stimulating my neurological center to
get my attention. I felt I was receiving more energy.

Anne was coming again. We discussed many topics as she
worked on me. Her comments always seemed to combine
physical health with my thoughts on spiritual health. For
instance, when we talked about fasting and meditation, she
explained that fasting is good to cleanse the body in order to
balance energy, in order for our bodies to operate at optimal
levels. She felt meditation rested the body to let the body come
in touch with its higher self, its soul. I shared how Mother
Mary repeats often at apparition sites "to fast and pray."

I now understood this two-fold reason for fasting is
probably Mary's reason for repeating the message so often. If
we empty our bodies in sacrifice, through fasting, it teaches us
mortification, which we can offer up to bring peace to the
world. Fasting also empties ourselves so the outside forces of
God's energies can better invade us. + Giving up food can be
done with prayer so that we become receptive to the
nourishment from God. Fasting can teach us that we do not
live by bread alone, but in union with God.

February 19, 1995. + I was awakened and began viewing
a scene of a desert. In time, a sprout started coming up out of
the ground in the desert scene. When the sprout reached
several inches above the earth it began to open, to bloom.
Slowly, the bud turned into a flower. I was overwhelmed with
a feeling of God's presence. I felt God was telling me my faith

133

had blossomed.

Anne worked on me again that afternoon. I told her about my vision of the flower. She said, "I bet it was a lotus." This opened the conversation about visions and she shared that she also experienced visions. I asked, "Do you have a hard time interpreting them?" She replied, "You get used to the language." I asked, "Why can't Spirit just tell us instead of all the symbols?" She replied, "Symbols are a universal language. Anyone, anywhere, can relate to pictures." We talked about my writings. She asked if she could read them.

As usual, I took plenty of books to read on vacation, several of them were in line with my re-occurring experiences. I shouldn't have been surprised. It seems God always sends the exact books to confirm and affirm what I'm thinking about. This time was no exception. I had several books to read on the energies of God, and several books on meditation.

I wanted to read more on meditation because I felt God wanted me to write more on this spiritual type of prayer. I meditate when reading, when I pray, and when I'm awakened at night with visions, but I was curious to read more on deep meditation by someone who teaches the subject. In *Sensing Your Hidden Presence*, written by Ignacio Larranaga, O.F.M. Cap, the author explained in simple language how to meditate. His explanation was in keeping with what Anne had recommended in quieting the body so that it could heal.

It is through spiritual meditation that an individual can become transformed to share in the family of God. In meditation I have been deluged with electrical jolts, which I believe are inspirations from the Holy Spirit. I have learned through the Holy Spirit's assistance to share in the intimacy of Jesus, to share in His greatness by learning and living His Word. When I experience the power of God regularly it's easy for me to share and give it away. I understand that charity should not be a mechanical act, but an overflowing of gathered treasures of the heart. I believe the call to be a Christian is nothing more than living our life with the emotions and attitudes of Jesus. I know we need to learn to live as Jesus did.

February 22, 1995. I witnessed lots of Light. + Then I saw a movie screen with lots of motion and action going across. The scene was like a movie in fast forward. Then suddenly the screen was filled with the words "The End." I began to cry because I thought God was answering my prayer and letting me know that my manuscript was finished. (It was several weeks later before I learned the correct interpretation of this vision.)

In the morning, when I shared with Erv I told him I felt a sadness. I had enjoyed the adventure of writing for God. I'd had many months of spontaneous exhilaration. I knew I'd miss my visions, my personal communications.

February 24, 1995. + I experienced a very strong electrical jolt. Light. Lots of Light for a long time. I was thrilled that I was still getting visions. Then I saw what I thought was a scroll being unrolled. I saw my name and many names being added to it. The scroll was then turned over. I felt immersed in joy and thanksgiving. I felt God was sharing with me a private revelation. My name was being added to the scroll of eternal life. So private I was never going to tell anyone. This was strictly for me.

When Anne came later that day she returned my manuscript. She said, "I'm supposed to follow you home." I was elated. "How do you know?" I exclaimed. She answered, "Jesus, spoke to me as I read your work. He wants me to teach you how to use your hands to do healing work." I knew instantly that was why I had seen my name being added to the scroll. It was the scroll with the name of workers for God." We decided she would come in April. She suggested I gather a group of individuals who would also be interested in learning. She would begin by teaching reflexology. I could hardly wait.

While on vacation I also read *Invaded by God* written by George A, Malonery, S.J. Reading this priest's definition of the energies of love and God added confirmation to my new adventure. I loved his comments about energies of God.

He wrote: "The doctrine of the Greek Fathers concerning grace primarily as God as uncreated energies of love has much to teach us. The early Fathers lived daily in the mystery of the triune God through experiencing God as energies of love. They knew they could never know or experience the essence of God, which always remained unknowable and incomprehensible to created man. But they knew from Holy Scripture that God does communicate Himself to man in a new knowing and a new participation through His energies. These energies are God's mode of existing in relationship to His created world, especially to man. These energies are not things, but they are truly God, Himself a Gift.

With the Divine energies always surrounding us and lovingly calling us to respond to God's Word living within us and within the context of our existential life, we reach our highest development in the continued cooperation with God's energy presence. When we continuously co-operate with God's grace His divine uncreated energies manifested to us in the context of our daily lives, we enter into the process of theosis or divinization, which is the total integration of the body-soul-spirit relationships of man with God. This is the end of God's creation of man as His masterpiece, endowed with an orientation to grow daily into the image and likeness of God that is Jesus Christ."

Back home. March 16, 1995. + I saw the eye very clearly. Then tears streaming from the eye. Then I saw blood dripping from a wound of a hand that I knew to be Christ's. I saw people laying hands on individuals. I knew I was being shown that this was what He expected of me. Another abundance of Light, wide, wide Light. The Light radiated in and out, feeling very intense. I then saw the face of Jesus, clearly enough to see His mustache. His face faded away with the Light.

I was thrilled, scared, confused, and wondered how I would ever be able to live up to what He was calling me to do.

April 9, 1995. + I saw a couple of lambs. One white, one black. Hands were putting headbands on the lambs. The kinds of headbands infants wear. Then I saw babies in a crib with toys. I felt confused.

After thinking about the scene, I realized He was showing me that His lambs learn like a baby learns. He knows how frightened I am in thinking about this new adventure. I felt He was letting me know I was going to be learning like a baby learns and that it would be fun.

April 10, 1995. + I saw a female with a flower on her shoulder, standing on a stage, turning around proudly. I realized it was me. I had earned my flower. Then I saw an eye crying, crying lots of tears. I knew He wanted me to do His will proudly, but I would be sharing in His cross and His sufferings.

April 20, 1995. This evening our prayer group received a message, the beginning of many profound messages. Jesus spoke through one of our members. I'll explain.

For me, it began that afternoon with a call from the Christian bookstore telling me the book I had ordered was in. I had hurriedly stopped at the bookstore on my way to church. When the saleswoman handed me *God Calling*, a book of messages that Jesus dictated for the world to two women in England, I remembered that Jane had suggested it during a recent phone conversation.

Before going into church, I sat in my car and began to read. I had read only a few pages when I thought, "How perfect. This message will be good to open our prayer group with tonight."

As we sat around a table I read the message Jesus gave to the two listeners in England.

I had just finished reading the message when one of our members, whom I noticed had been acting strangely by drumming her fingers on the table suddenly said, "I have a message for us." She began speaking in a soft voice with words unlike any she would normally use or that we had ever heard her say. I remember hearing a long message, a real "God Message," but I was so in awe I only remember, +"*My*

Heavenly Text

daughters. I am here with you. I am standing on the table in your midst. Know that...
"*Have faith. Trust. Pray.*"

We felt a powerful presence and continued our prayers. After we ended our prayers we turned to our friend with questions, "What was that?" "Where did that come from?" "What did it feel like?" "How did you feel?" "What did you say?"

She had no idea what she had said and all of us were in such a state of shock that we remembered only the beginning and end statements. We were filled with amazement, filled with emotion, and filled with thanksgiving. Our hour of prayers had reflected those feelings.

April 21, 1995. Anne arrived at my home in Columbia. She had informed me ahead of time that she would stay several days. She would put on a two-day seminar and also take private appointments.

I had returned home full of enthusiasm about my foot improvement and shared my good news with many. I had organized a dozen women who were anxious to spend eight hours on Saturday and Sunday, learning alternative healing techniques.

The seminar was two intense days of learning, of being worked on and working on others. We all bonded in our efforts to grow in knowledge about energies within our bodies. Anne taught us reflexology, which is a good basic introduction for beginners on how energy runs throughout the body. Anne's method of reflexology incorporates ancient techniques derived from the study of Meridians and Acupuncture. She also demonstrated some acupressure and assured us she would return if we wanted more education on her expertise.

There were twelve of us working on each other's feet. I thought about Christ statement when he washed the twelve apostles' feet. "At the moment you do not know what I am doing, but later you will understand." I wondered if His gesture could have been teaching us of our own innate healing

138

potential. My mind was a continuous whirl of thoughts.

Monday morning while Anne and I were having coffee my doorbell rang. I wondered who would be so early at my door. I went to the door in my robe and there stood a young man, a neighbor. Asim is from Pakistan and lives with his family on our street. He attends college here in Columbia. He often comes to see me. He said, "Good morning Miss Nancy, I just wanted to say Hi! I've missed seeing you. Can we talk?" I informed him I was busy, had company, had a busy day ahead of me and suggested we make it another time. I thanked him for his interest. When I came in I expressed to Anne that the occurrence seemed odd so early in the morning.

Anne left for appointments and said she would return by noon for other appointments that would be coming to my house. She had brought a dozen or so books on alternative healing techniques so I spent most of the morning reading.

That afternoon my home was a buzz with many smiles, hugs, and thank you from the grateful individuals coming and going. Anne seems to have a way of profoundly changing people's lives. She truly helps heal all kinds of wounds, of the body and of the heart.

When Bonnie came she asked, "What's today's date?" I said, "You've got me. Too much going on around here this week." I looked at my calendar and responded, "It's the 25th, oh my, it's the 25th today and tomorrow." I promptly brought the calendar into view. She and Anne were as amazed as I to see two 25ths on my calendar. Never had I, in my 53 years seen such a thing. So strange. We laughed. The calendar happened to be an angel calendar, pictures of angels on each month. Someone had given it to me for a Christmas gift that seemed to make this happening even more intriguing. Was this a +? Then I noticed the picture of the angel for the month of April was called The Annunciation. That's strange, too. I know March 25 is the feast of the Annunciation. We all decided computers don't make errors on pages on calendars and that I should try to call the publisher of the calendar (Random House) and check on this mistake.

Heavenly Text

I called immediately. The woman I spoke with in customer service could not give me much information because they had destroyed all of the extra calendars for '95 and were in the process of printing their '96 calendars. She remarked, "I think it's really impossible for that to have happened. Are you sure? We have had no other calls with that problem." I later called every store in town to try to locate a duplicate calendar to compare and was informed all had been sold or disposed of. I was beginning to think the calendar was a real physical +.

That afternoon as I sat on my screened porch reading. I picked up one of Anne's books, *Therapeutic Touch* written by Delores Krieger RN, Ph.D. I instantly knew that this book was also describing God's gift. This technique is used in hundreds of nursing schools, and hospitals around the world to provide comfort to those in pain, anxiety, tension or stress. In reading it I realized once again how my hands, my energies, had helped Pam's face balance its energies. I knew deep inside that all of the different healing techniques that I had been hearing and reading about was the same thing - God's power and energy. I began to feel the flame of love. + God was confirming that He was educating me in numerous ways on His energy that surrounds and abides in all of us.

As I sat on the screened porch gazing into the woods, I thanked God for the abundance of information. I shared my enthusiasm with a bird close by, "God is teaching me what you probably already know." Before I knew it there were dozens of birds, and several squirrels all gathering in close, chirping and squeaking away. It was a very profound feeling. I had given out energy to the woods and it was coming back. + I felt I now understood John's comment: "If you belonged to the world, the world would love you as its own." (John 15:19)

Shortly, Anne came out on the porch between appointments and remarked, "What is all the noise? What is going on out here?" I shared that I was feeling like St. Francis. We looked over the deck and there below us several deer had also arrived. Anne explained, "I believe all the animals are sensing the energy here today. Everything God created is

140

energy and energy responds to energy." She then began sharing a Native American story which states deer are medicine of delight.

I felt on a high from all my animal friends. This was not my first animal high or my last. Remember the bird I wrote about when I returned from Conyers? + Well, that bird, or its look- alike, kept coming to the window as I first typed the above information. Powerful. +

That evening after Erv arrived home I was preparing dinner, when the doorbell rang. I went to the door and there stood the young Pakistani man again, with his dog at his side. He looked at me with intense eyes and said, "Can I have a drink of water?" I replied, "Your house is just two doors away. Why don't you go to your own home?" I felt submerged in his eyes. He continued looking longingly and said, "Please give me a drink of water." I thought, this is very, very, strange. I returned to my kitchen and got him a glass of water. I announced to Erv and Anne as I passed through, "Something strange is going on here."

When I returned to the porch I felt Asims' strong concern, his anxiety, his eagerness to communicate something to me. I motioned for him to sit on the step and I sat saying, "Sit down here. Tell me what is going on with you." He poured water into his hand and offered it to his dog. The dog quickly lapped it up. The young man's eyes were glistening, as if filled with tears. I was entirely taken by surprise and shocked when he said, "The clouds have spoken. The world is full of evil. The earth is about to erupt." + I softly replied, "I know." The moment was one of unspeakable profoundness, awareness, and a deep mystical knowing. + I asked him why he came to my house to tell me this. He said, "I just knew I was supposed to. I knew inside." I told him I call those God messages. He readily agreed. He went on with, "What can I do? Nobody believes me." I told him to pray. I asked if he believed in Jesus. "Oh, yes. I live my life for him." I suggested we pray, that we both pray about the information he had delivered. He looked at me with love and got up saying, "You have filled me with joy. Thank you." And he strolled up the driveway.

I came in sharing the profound experience with Anne and Erv. Both agreed it was very unusual. Anne remarked, "Sounds like something Blackhawk would say. A very educated young man you have living close by." I locked the experience in my heart. I wondered if God was asking me to write more about the end times, the end of this era.

That evening after dinner, Erv had a meeting, and Anne and I had a wonderful, meaningful visit. We shared many stories. Later that night when I went to bed I had a vision or a lucid dream, I'm not positive what it was because it was different. I experienced lots of Light, over- layered figures of Light that I barely could distinguish. It was very hard to describe what I was seeing. Lots of Light, Light, Light. + When I told Anne at breakfast the next morning she commented, "I think it means you are learning all the layers of healing with Light." Her words felt right to me and resonated deeply. I recalled the vision of March 16th of people laying-on-hands.

Then the next day individuals began to arrive for their scheduled treatments with Anne. It was another wonderful time. Anne worked on me several times throughout her stay and she was as thrilled as I in the continued improvement of my foot.

I sneaked out around noon to a near-by store to purchase a shower gift because I had told my friends that I would attend their bridal shower the next day. I returned home with the gift. As I wrapped it, I looked at the invitation to see where and when. The invite said, Tuesday the 25th of April. I looked at my calendar and I had written the time on Wednesday the 25th of April. This was Tuesday, so the shower was in progress as I stood looking at my calendar. I realized another mix-up because of my unusual calendar. I thought, "Obviously, God wanted me home today."

That evening I called with my regrets and excuses to the

hostess and she immediately exclaimed, "Are you all right? We were worried when you didn't show up today." I thanked her for the invitation and tried to explain the calendar date crazies and she laughing said, "It's really strange. All the seats at all the tables were full. There were twenty-five here. I don't know where we would have put you if you came." I knew again in my heart it was a strong + that I was supposed to remain home that day.

As friends arrived throughout the day I shared my April 25th mix-up dates and there were many comments. One woman viewing the calendar exclaimed, "Oh, my heavens!" Anne returned with, "Perfect comment for an angel calendar." We had fun with the experience of the two dates both days.

That evening after dinner, Erv retired early, exhausted from a full day's work at Habitat for Humanity. He is now supervisor for the weekday crew. His days are filled with physical labor. Understandably, he tires more easily than he did working at his sales job.

Anne and I sat on the screened porch enjoying each other's company and reliving the experiences of the last five days. Suddenly, out of the corner of my eye, I saw an object hovering over a light on the deck. At first I thought it was a bat but then realized it was a huge beautiful butterfly. Anne remarked, "I bet there is another one close by." Almost instantly another one appeared. I reveled in the moment that felt like a gift from God. It felt like He was letting us know we were being thought of. I wondered if it was normal for butterflies to be out at night in Missouri, at 10pm at the end of April. It was a very special feeling. +

Shortly thereafter, Anne announced she was leaving immediately. I couldn't believe she was leaving at 10pm. I tried to talk her into waiting until morning. We went upstairs and she gathered her already packed bags. I had the strangest feeling when she said, "I know when it's time to go. I'm finished here for now. I'll be back when you need me." I didn't want to let her go. It had been such a powerful five days. I felt sadness but also joy as she drove up my driveway. She was like an angel fleeing in the night.

The next morning, as I drank my coffee, I picked up my Bible and headed for my porch. I opened it and began in John where my marker had indicated I had stopped a few days before. I nearly spilled my coffee as I shivered when I read, "If you only knew what God is offering and who it is saying to you; 'Give me a drink of water', you would have been the one to ask, and he would have given you living water." + I was overcome with an unbelievably profound remembrance of the neighbor uttering those words on my porch.

I instantly remembered the vision of April 16, and 19th. + God definitely was getting my attention. All of these visions seemed to be referring to messages from Revelation.

Later I picked up the book, *Mary's Message to the World*, written by Anne Kirkwood that Anne had left for me to read. It seemed appropriate to turn to the last chapter, which I discovered from the index was Jesus' explanation of the wording and meaning of Revelation in Scripture.

I nearly dropped the book when I read: *Your connection to God is coming with the clouds. Clouds denote the thoughts of man.* +

I had heard, "The clouds have spoken" from the young man on my porch. Jesus was definitely present in that event. I felt it then. I know it now. +

I continued to read: *Every eye is speaking of the inner eye, the eye that allows you to see the truth.* +

A compelling message about the eye that I always see. + I literally came unglued with chills and tears. I whispered, "God, are you telling me you want me to write more about the scriptures in Revelation? That really scares me."

I read on. *The scroll represents the history of man. There is writing on both sides of the scroll because you are at the end of an era.* +

I recalled the vision of February 24, when I saw the scroll turned over. Was the scroll vision telling me of the end? In the vision of February 22, I'd seen the words "The End." Now it all began to make sense. The end did not mean the end of my books, but the end of the era in which we now live.

I read on: *When John took the little scroll and ate it, the taste was like honey in the mouth, but bitter in the stomach. This means when you know of the end times and are prophesying to others the news will be sweet in their mouth. But when they think on the message they will turn against you. The role you are playing will be bittersweet one. It will bring fame and infamy.* + I recalled the vision of April 10 when Jesus was crying tears. + He was preparing me with that vision, again telling me I was going to be helping to carry His cross. He knew what a challenge this all would be for me.

I read on: *The Saints and all people are now offering prayers for you on earth. The amount of prayers sound like thunder, lightning, earthquakes.* +

I thought of all my electrical jolts of lightning and visions of earthquakes. "So they truly are prayers from heaven. Thanks, God."

I read on: *Now as you read, there is a multitude in white robes.* +

I knew this woman and I both were experiencing many of the same things because I had recently started to occasionally see bodies of light in robes that I knew were Spirits.

I was finally grasping the meaning of my recent visions. God had been giving them one right after another. I must have reread this information a dozen times as I trembled, cried, and prayed. I was overwhelmed. I was afraid I couldn't do what he wanted me to do.

I knew, without a doubt, Jesus wanted me to write about the end times of the era in which we now are living. I'd read many messages from Mother Mary talking about this era ending, and now I was being told to write about them. I was filled with emotion. I thought, "Why did this all ever begin with me. Where am I headed now? God sure works in mysterious ways, and yet in clear ways, if one keeps alert and pays attention."

It was three months before I saw the young Pakistani man again. He came for a visit. He began to talk about the day he had visited with his dog. He explained, "That day was very profound. I don't know how to explain it, but I felt like Jesus took over my body on that day." I replied, "Maybe He did." I shared the occurrences that had happened to me. We were both in awe. He has since moved and I miss his visits.

April 27, 1995. + I had a vivid dream. There was a large gathering of individuals. I knew this occurrence was very important. I didn't remember anything else.

I woke up and relived the dream. I remembered my vision of April 8 and the lambs. Could the placing of the bands on the lambs be a symbol of the marking of the seal on the foreheads of the chosen? (Rev. 7:3) Did the children in the cribs symbolize the gathering of His children because of the end times? Had God been trying to get the message through to me multiple times?

April 28, 1995. + This night I awoke around 2am with an intense internal voice speaking to me. Immediately, I was compelled to get up and write down the message. The message was full of meaning. It filled me with joy and delight. It was a strong, strong interior voice that said: + *"This is an ancient story of wisdom. When a man speaks words of truth they go forth as thoughts of good. When a man speaks words of truth they come back to him as truth. The story goes that each one is to pass on what they know of the truth. Jesus' words were nothing but truth. It is why His words go forth from generation to generation. Anyone who reads scripture openly eventually hears the truth. When one hears the truth it is easy to say, "I know that I know."* (Powerful and profound words for me to hear.)

I pray, "Dear Lord, as I walk this road of learning your truths I pray you enlighten me, guide me, encourage me, strengthen me, help me. Let my love and your love be one. Let my words be your words. I love you. I vow to try to always place my attitudes, thoughts, and deeds, in a straight line with you. I feel I am advancing in spirit and truth, but I need to do more. Good thoughts. Happy thoughts. Loving thoughts. Thoughts of gratitude. In happenings. In coincidences. In visions. In dreams. In voices. In "all." I want to become one with you and you with me. I know the universal goal is for us all to become one family. I believe this family of ours will come about in a worldwide thought pattern when we all think in terms of "all" as our connection with you. I now know, really know, it is imperative that I learn to control my attitudes and my beliefs in order to control my thoughts."

April 29, 1995. + I had a vision of glowing hands of Light with the eye in the center. I saw a lot of Light and lots of movement. Hands appeared to be around a baby being born. Hands were around ill people. Hands were around many, many people. I then saw a rooftop that looked like my house and saw Light entering and exiting. I had the feeling of receiving more energy, more strength, more knowing. Questions popped into my mind. "Is this house being filled with energy?" "Getting ready for healings?"

April 30, 1995. I heard clearly another ancient wisdom lesson. I immediately got up to write it down. Again a strong, strong, interior voice: +*"There are many levels of healing. 1. Realizing there is healing. 2. Trying to perform the healings. 3. Connecting (believing) in the healings. 4. Actually assisting (being present for) the healings. When one is in thought with God, grounded to the earth, grounded with the universe, healings happen because all is on one equal plane. Healings can be thought of as a strike of lightning going from the top to the bottom through the healer, into the healed, into the earth and back again. It's nothing more than the circle of chakras getting bigger and bigger. A healer is a vessel for God to work through."*

I knew deep inside God was, without a doubt, preparing me and calling me for healing work. I prayed for strength and courage.

May 2, 1995. I received a very interesting note from my friend Sylvie. It read. Dear Nancy, I need to give you the phone number of the mother of a friend of mine. Her name is Eileen. I don't know why, but I need to do it. She is a retired nurse who has been to Yugoslavia and Conyers and is very involved in Catholicism. You may never call her, but I need to give it to you.

It sounded like a strong + to me. I picked up the phone and dialed. I began speaking to Eileen, "This is a strange phone call because I don't know why I'm calling you." I shared the name of the person who gave me the number and Eileen did not know who she was. I asked if her daughter lived in Columbia. She said, "No." I asked, "Do you believe in God Messages?" She replied, "Absolutely." I continued, "I've been writing a book about apparition sites. Does that connect with you?" "Oh, yes. We've had a prayer group for 25 years. One night after church, because of a terrible snowstorm, seven families had to spend the night in a home next to the church because we were unable to get our cars out of the parking lot. That night all of our children, who were very young, began speaking in tongues. We didn't know what was going on. We decided to start a prayer group. We have continued to meet over these 25 years and now Mother Mary is giving us messages. You do know we are in the end times..." + "Yes," I replied, "This seems to be the week God has told me this message in many different ways. I think this means I am supposed to visit and write about your prayer group. Would that be all right?"

She informed me that they meet on Tuesdays. "Where do you live?" I asked. She explained on the Iowa-Illinois border. I knew this would be about five or six hours away. I commented, "Let me get my thoughts together on all of this. I'm a bit overwhelmed at the moment and can't think straight.

I'll call you back."

I sat by my desk, mystified, exalted, and in somewhat a state of shock realizing I was going to be writing about another Mother Mary experience. Powerful, powerful. + I knew Jesus and Mary were leading me again.

Shortly, Erv arrived home. I asked if he wanted to go with me on another interesting adventure. He declined. I called a member of my prayer group, Dottie, and asked if she would go with me. We decided to go on May 16.

May 4, 1995. + I was a participant in a workshop - A Spiritual Journey for the Cancer Patient - that was held at a local hospital. The day was very meaningful. It consisted of various speeches, a panel, and open questioning. I was on a panel of survivors of cancer with four other individuals who were cancer patients, some in remission. I represented, through Pam's words, a death from cancer. When I spoke of Pam and our circumstances I was led by the Spirit to speak about my new interest in Touch and Healing with our hands. Afterwards eight individuals approached me to sign up, if there was ever another class. I thought to myself, "I need to call Anne. It's time for another training visit."

That evening our prayer group met. All seven of us were present. I shared the interesting events of the week. We began to pray. Suddenly, we received another message from Jesus through one of our members. It was a spellbinding mystical happening. We felt it in our hearts. Chills, tears, and energy, were flowing abundantly. Afterwards we discussed the message. The following is the culmination of what we put together from all that we heard.

+"*My daughters, I am with you. I am in your midst. I'm here to give you hope and strength to do my will. I pour my love out to you. I ask you to pour it out unto others. I am sending the Holy Spirit upon you. You will have power. My power. Know that I am with you. I love you as you love me.*"

After hearing the message we continued to sit quietly, overcome with emotion, speechless for a period of time and

Heavenly Text

then we continued our prayers. It was our custom to sit around the table, holding hands while we prayed. When we finished praying that evening our hands were mysteriously raised into the air. Wonderment filled us all as we reviewed what we had heard and what had happened. I wondered how many would heed the call. The evening certainly fit with my week.

I later wrote, "The wind blows wherever it pleases; you hear its sound, but you cannot tell where it comes from or where it is going. That is how it is with all who are born of the Spirit." (John 3:7-9) This describes how I feel. God is blowing me in the wind. I know not where I am being taken, where I am being led, where I am going. Only God knows. He seems to have me going at an accelerated pace. I have heard God's call. God is educating me. I believe it is through my prayer and my surrender that God teaches me. I constantly ask for guidance to grow spiritually and to help me understand. God is constantly giving us all opportunities to receive His Spirit. I'm learning that one receives the Spirit by uniting soul, mind, and heart with Him. As my life unfolds, I think only of Jesus. How He was led. How He followed. How He obeyed. I pray to learn to adhere to His ways and His thoughts. I pray to become like Him. I've given Him my heart.

I know God is the breath of life. (Spiritus in Latin is breath.) I know if we state we are truly seeking God, God finds us. I feel His presence. I feel His attraction. I feel His power. I feel I am emptying myself and becoming one with Him.

His Divine power is the power that propels each of us. His Divine energy, if we are open to it, is what propels us on into deeper realization of His will. This energy flows in and through us. I feel I have activated this energy of my soul. I feel immersed and energized by His power. Each time I reach a new level of relationship with God, He seems to propel me deeper. For me, it's an endless searching, probing into a deeper purity of heart, an ever increasing union with the Holy Spirit. God is always one step ahead of me. He keeps inviting me to new levels of surrender, faith and love.

I pray, "Thank You, God. Thank you for including me in this journey of gifts that I am enjoying. I now realize that over these past two years I've been learning the gifts of the Holy Spirit. I know this is what you want. Thanks for not giving up on me. It has been overwhelmingly rewarding. I wouldn't trade my experiences for anything. I know this is why I'm now finding peace and joy. All of the wonderful, amazing, mystical experiences have been powerful and abundantly full of your love. I'm working on loving you more and more. I now know we can all experience you here on earth. Thank You, I love you."

"Anyone who is joined to the Lord is one spirit with him." (1 Cor.12: 4-11)

Gift of the Giver

The more I open my heart and unite my thoughts with God, the more gifts come. I'm beginning to realize this could go on forever.

I know God is leading me to deeper thoughts on healings, the Gift of all gifts, from the Giver of all gifts. I'm no different from anyone else in my personal searching. Searching of the human heart is common to us all. I want to emphasize the all. God is for us all. No individual, no race, no religion is excluded. Anyone who thinks Jesus Christ is just for themselves or their religion or one way of life doesn't know the God I know. I have a larger view, one that envisions God as head of all. He created us all. He believes in us all. He is watching us all struggle to come home to Him. There are many paths within our grasp to reach Him.

Throughout centuries, various individuals, tensions and rigidity have created many separations in God's plan. We need to learn to let our minds get out of the way so that our hearts can lead us. I believe our hearts need to be awakened to an oneness with Him and each other. Love thy neighbor as thyself implies genuine love, true unconditional love. To live by true love from the heart is a daily challenge.

I feel it is imperative that each one of us learns the meaning of the words responsibility, reverence, integrity, compassion, and love, instead of insisting on specific beliefs of a specific religion. Religious rituals are nothing more than a means from God to entice us, to educate us, to bring us to one thought with Him. Since I am Catholic I have grown from the

152

lessons handed down though the years from my forefathers, but I also have questioned and studied on my own.

In the Catholic Church, healings were foremost in the thoughts of our forefathers when praying for the sick. Everyone followed the examples that Jesus taught until about 400 A.D. when Pope Innocent declared oil to be consecrated and used only by priests in anointing the sick and praying for the dead. An interest in mysticism and supernatural healings persisted, but it was thought by the majority that healings occurred only "to" and "for" the chosen, mostly mystics and saints. After the Council of Trent in the 1700's there was still another edict issued that forbade individuals other than priests to anoint the sick. Since the 1960's, Pope John XXIII and Vatican II, a new atmosphere of openness between the clergy and the people has emerged. More Catholics have been experiencing an awakening to the practice of laying-on-of-hands by religious and lay persons. In the Mass at the sign of peace, the extension of our hands to each other is a simple gesture sharing this Spirit/energy.

Many of us attend church regularly, attend workshops, attend classes, get degrees, read books, and continually search for meaning. But how many of us actually succeed in transforming our life into a life that imitates Christ's? A life for our soul. A life beyond death. Isn't this the purpose behind every spiritual tradition?

Life and death are mysteries. Jesus' life was full of mysteries. He entered the world mysteriously. He entered into the mysteries of life and lived them. He invites us all to do the same. I feel submerged in His mystery. Our Lord did not come to take away the responsibilities for ourselves. He came to teach us to follow Him. He came to empower us with His power. To follow Christ means to become responsible for our lives: in living, in dying, in sadness, in joy, in reaching out to others, in becoming one with Him. Peace does not mean security with the world. It means peace from within.

As I search for this peace, I'm led by deep intuitive nudges. Going to Iowa was one of those times.

Heavenly Text

May 16, 1995. Dottie S. and I went to visit the prayer group in Iowa. It was raining when we left at 6am. I really dislike driving in the rain but within the hour the sun came out.

We arrived at noon, as the women were gathering at the humble home of Eileen. We were warmly greeted and my mind began to twirl with the thought of "Why are we here?" Thirteen women had come on this day, each bringing a dish to share for lunch. Conversation was cordial and enlightening as we ate.

The prayer group told us that on certain occasions they receive messages from Mother Mary and that one of their daughters receive messages from Jesus through automatic writing. A couple of the women had been to Medjugorje and shared those stories with us.

The group shared their interest in the birth of a white buffalo in southern Wisconsin, which some of them had been to see. Native Americans feel the buffalo, named Miracle, is a sacred sign of a new era, an era of reconciliation among races and respect for the earth. Apparently many years ago, a beautiful woman appeared to an Indian. She told him that a new era was coming and explained they would know when this era was near at hand when a white buffalo was born. The women explained that the buffalo would turn from white, to brown, to yellow, to black, and back to white again. This would be a sign the new era would be upon the earth. As she departed she walked away as a white buffalo. (By 2002 the buffalo's coat had turned three colors.)

After lunch we gathered in the living room and prayers began. We had informed them we would be leaving around three because we wanted to make the trip home the same day. Before the time for us to depart, they asked if they could have community prayer over us. Not actually knowing what they meant I replied, "Of course, we'd love it." They gathered around, each laying their hands on me. They began praying. Since I had never found myself in a situation like this, I was somewhat puzzled, questioning the validity, yet feeling a presence of power as they prayed.

Heavenly Text

Several women immediately began speaking in tongues. Two other women began interpreting these messages. One of the women had the gift of visualization and began sharing comforting messages. I heard one of them say, "You are surrounded in Light. I see you in a picture frame full of Light which tells me you are doing exactly what is expected of you in this time frame of your life."

More words that seemed to be from God quickly followed. +"*You are mine.*" "*I have chosen you.*" "*Your writings are for my honor and glory.*" "*It's your actions not your words that please me.*" "*You are doing this for my sheep.*" "*Many young people will be helped.*" "*You are to study the messages from Medjugorje.*" "*Your daughter is here with you.*"

I was very moved, bewildered and elated, but the last comment brought the tears rolling down my cheeks as I recalled Pam's words, "Jesus told me last night this will help many, many people."

They continued, "I was with you on your trip here and I will be with you on your return trip." +

Someone asked, "Do you have any questions?" My mind went blank. If this truly was a direct line to Jesus what should I ask? I was stunned and couldn't think of a thing - nothing. Finally I uttered, "Is my book about finished?" The answer was "*In my time. You will know.*" + They continued praying over me for a bit and then all became quiet.

Next, they prayed over Dottie S. I was still processing my messages, but remembered hearing more prayers uttered to her, more speaking in tongues, and "I see a crucifix, a tabernacle spinning. I believe you are to spread increased devotion to the Blessed Sacrament." "You are a child of God." "Help foster and spread the news of no extreme music and dancing in churches." Someone asked Dottie if she had any questions. She asked, "Will I ever speak in tongues?" They then prayed over both of us, requesting the gift of tongues to be given to us.

Good-byes were said, hugs given, and we departed. As I began driving the long trip home I immediately asked Dottie to write down everything we had heard and experienced so I

155

wouldn't forget.

Since neither Dottie S. nor I had a prior experience of the interpretation of tongues we were questioning the authenticity of the experience. Yet we both were deeply touched by the occurrence. Dottie questioned, "Why did this happen to us?" I commented, "Trust me. In time we will know. This is how God messages work. I still can't believe I couldn't think of any questions to ask? Do you suppose this is going to happen to our prayer group?" Our discussion continued along these lines.

After we were on the road about an hour the sky began to look threatening. Not just a few rain clouds but dark, low, pitch black, strange looking clouds were rolling in. My body began to dread the rest of the drive. Intense thunder and lighting soon began. It began to rain so hard I could barely see the road. In order to find the courage to keep going I kept repeating to myself the words I'd heard earlier, "*I will be with you on your return trip.*" +

It was a terrible storm, with no end in sight. With water everywhere and getting higher and higher we were concerned about flash flooding. We could hardly find the dozens of turns we had made coming. I kept hoping we'd see a motel or find a place to stop. Eventually, I found a spot to pull over to the side of the road for a few minutes just to rest my shoulders and eyes. The lightning and thunder was furious. We were definitely feeling and seeing the power of God. Suddenly, the entire inside of our car strangely lit up. (+?) It wasn't like lightning--we heard no crack of thunder. There was a dead silence. Dottie commented, "Do you think that was a sign?" I said, "I sure hope so. I want to think we have some protection here. I'm scared to death." We got back on the road and proceeded on. It was around 8 pm when we saw a sign indicating a turn to Hannibal, Mo. I said, "I'm turning, it's a few miles out of our way but maybe we can find a motel." When we got into Hannibal we stopped at a couple of motels before we found an available room.

As we checked into the motel I noticed the evening's local newspaper on the counter read, "Flood gates being anchored

Heavenly Text

into place as water quickly rises." I thought, "Great. Now we'll be washed away by the Mississippi River." (Downtown Hannibal is right next to the river.) The room we were given was upstairs and I commented to Dottie, "We might wake up in the morning and look out and see our car floating, but for now we will be dry." We called our husbands and told them we'd decided to stay in Hannibal. When we viewed the weather channel we heard the weatherman report that the rain had been coming down an inch an hour.

The thunder and lightning was constant all night. Dottie woke up at 5:45am and immediately turned on the TV to check the weather radar. We could see an open clear space right around us extending to Columbia. Seeing the small clearing I said, "There's our chance. Let's get out of here and maybe we'll make it home before the next deluge." About two hours later, as I drove into Columbia it was again beginning to pour down exceedingly hard. I don't remember ever being so glad to pull into my garage. It continued raining all day, a total of eleven inches in 24 hours for Missouri, which resulted in flooding for the Midwest for the second spring in a row.

During the night I had had a vision: + I was viewing the world once again from above, and it seemed the world was falling apart everywhere. + I told Dottie, "I'm afraid this weather is the beginning of many terrible disasters that are going to befall the globe in the months ahead."

I could hardly wait to talk to Father Mike. When I told him of the speaking in tongues and the interpretations given he commented, "We call that prophesy. It is definitely a gift. You were fortunate to find yourself in that situation. I hope you had lots of questions to ask." "Nope," I replied, "I was so taken back, so questioning, so in awe, that for a change I just listened instead of talking." He suggested I read (1 Cor.14:23-25).

After reading the quote, the visit to the prayer group made more sense. God had taught me another lesson. Dottie and I were definitely initiates and God had wanted to impress on us the validity of His truths spoken in prophecy.

Heavenly Text

May 22, 1995. + A vision of a large eye, crying lots of tears. The scene lasted a long time. Lots of Light streamed towards me. I wondered what was in store.

May 28, 1995. + I again witnessed a view of the globe. The view zoomed in and I immediately recognized Alaska. I realized the problem was due west of the Alaska coastline. I had a sense of something terrible happening. The next day I discovered the vision took place during the time of a big earthquake on the Russian coastline.

June 13, 1995. + I was very confused when I clearly saw in a vision the words "Valore End." Then I saw a baby playing with toys. An adult was helping the baby. I thought this vision was telling me that I was learning like a baby.

When I saw Fr. Mike he looked up the wording in a Latin dictionary and found the lettering meant, "To be strong to the end." (John 13:13) So we decided I was being told to hang in there. God knows at times I get confused, perplexed, and doubtful.

Later I read in scripture, "You will be hated by man on account of my name; but the man who stands firm to the end will be saved." I was amazed at the correlation of all of the 13's on the thirteenth. Maybe the adult was Mother Mary helping this child-me. ("Thanks, God.")

June 14, 1995. + I was awakened with a strong electrical jolt. I saw hands and heard an internal voice saying, "*Use your hands.*" I then saw the Blessed Mother clearly in a vision. I replied, "I'm trying to learn. Please give me the courage, please lead the way."

That week I was introduced to the book, *Foxfire*, a book written in the later 1960ís,which is a collection of folklore and stories from the southern Appalachian Mountains. In it I read several articles on old time faith healers. The authors made it clear that they did not see any of the healings but only talked with the healers who were simple folks strong in their beliefs. These old time healers appeared to have faith in God and faith in themselves, and the tradition of healing was passed down through generations. They believed that it was through God that their words carried weight. These healers did not heal in tents. They did not accept money for their work. When asked to help they worked and prayed with their neighbors.

The following quote explains these healers' feelings. "I don't doctor it, I don't cure it, I'm used as a vessel of the Lord and He does the work and He does the cur'in. Do you understand what I mean? I just do the words and put faith in God and God does the work himself. He does the cur'in and the heal'in. It's not me that does it."

Usually these healers didn't reveal the words they used, but one lady shared her special words stating that maybe it would help when she was dead and gone. She stated she was a healer of burns. She would say the following verse as she passed her hand over the burn and blew the heat away from the burn and the body. "There came an angel from the East bringing frost and fire. In frost out fire. In the name of the father the Son and of the Holy Ghost."

The healers simply believed in the power of God with true faith, and claimed their healings. They reminded me of Jesus saying, "Daughter, your faith has made you well, go in peace, and be healed of your disease." (John 5:21-43)

("Thanks, God, this is the kind of healer I would like to be.")

June 19, 1995. + Another electrical jolt awakened me. I again saw the world falling apart. Lots of breaking away of land. Lots of water. It was disturbing to view.

July 3, 1995. + I saw myself. My hands working on peoples' feet, My hands holding individuals heads. My hands touching many people.

I knew God was again telling me to get more involved in healing. "I'm trying, God." I uttered. "Please lead and guide me."

The next day I was thrilled to hear about a nurse, Sandy. She teaches and uses Therapeutic Touch in our local hospital. The information came in a roundabout way via a note from someone in St. Louis. + I gave Sandy a call. She invited me to her home. We spent several hours together. The information she shared with me only heightened my knowing and understanding and was similar to what Anne had said.

I returned from Sandy's home loaded with more books to read. Also a package of information, including books on Reiki arrived from Anne. In the East, healing with hands is called Reiki (universal life energy) and has been used for centuries. Reiki was once considered a mystery and guarded and preserved by ancient cultures, available to few people, and mostly practiced by spiritual leaders. Then in the middle of the 19th century Dr. Mikas Usui, a monk in Japan began a search to understand the connection between the healing methods of Christ and the Buddha's ability to heal. His search brought him to America and he became a doctor of Theology. While meditating one day, he had a mystical experience that reawakened him to the knowledge of laying on of hands in a specific order to balance energies. He ran a private clinic in Japan and had phenomenal success with helping individuals heal. He emphasized that the important part of the practice is the dedication of one's life to help others. The practice continues to grow rapidly here and around the world.

I read day and night for a week. Once again reading was helping to build my knowledge and confidence in this new adventure. As I learned more about healings in many cultures, by many different people, I came to the realization that the gift of healing from God is ancient and universal, available to us all. This Spirit/energy is given many different names in different cultures and religions: **Holy Spirit**-Christian, **Chi**-Chinese, **Prana**-Hindu, **Man**-Kahuma, **Bioplasmic**- Russian, **Prneuma**-Greek, **Ka**-Egyptian, and on and on. There are common grounds among the many but the wordings, logistics, and beliefs are a little different. Just as all spiritual traditions teach similar laws to live by, they all have different names for their spiritual encounters - Kundalini, miracles, spiritual awakening, charismatic renewal and on and on.

It became more and more evident to me that we're all on the same search, with the same Spirit/energy, under the same leadership (God), to become one with the Creator, who also has many different names in many different cultures. Many agree that it is through compassion, willingness, and belief that we can all learn to share our hands with others to enhance health, to reduce pain, to promote wellness and wholeness, to bring peace to our souls.

July 10, 1995. + I was awakened by a strong electrical jolt. I felt I was receiving more grace, courage and confidence. Often one of these jolts precedes a special occurrence so my interest in the week ahead heightened.

July 13, 1995. + Sandy, the nurse, had invited me to join a group of individuals in administering various healing techniques to each other. They meet monthly at their homes. I arrived around 9am at Jeanne's, the location for the shared healing work. I was curious and anxious to see what the day would bring. Seven people came. I was the only one who had never tried any of my newly learned techniques on strangers. They made me feel welcomed. Jeanne put me at ease when she commented; "There are no right or wrong ways to help heal others with your hands." I was elated when she offered to demonstrate CranioSacral Therapy on me.

She explained that CranioSacral therapy is an osteopathic procedure, a manipulation technique, which helps improve the functioning of one's brain and spinal cord that helps the person heal within. As she began she immediately asked, "What's going on with your right ear?" I wondered why she asked, although I remembered Anne had once asked the same thing. Jeanne gently worked by simply placing her hands along my spine and on and around my head. I experienced the most relaxed feelings that I have ever encountered. When she was gently pressing on my ear she suddenly started crying, saying, "I feel something powerful is happening." I was introduced to the fact that Jeanne has the gift of visualizing and feeling correlating emotions. (I remembered the women in Iowa experiencing this in prayer.) Jeanne asked, "Did you live in a rural area? I answered, "Yes." She asked, "Has anything happened to you in a field? I see you lying in tall grass." I answered, "Not that I remember."

My heart started racing. As my heart raced and she began sharing her emotions I was puzzled. I became very warm and suddenly my body felt like the flame of God's love. + As I lay there and she continued to administer light touch to my head, I tried to remember my childhood. Why was this happening and why was she asking? She said, "I'll explain somatic emotional release to you later," and she continued with her therapy. By the time she finished I felt as if I could float off the table. The sensations were wonderful. I had never realized anyone could get this relaxed, much less me. I mentally put the therapy at the top of my list.

Jeanne then explained to me. "Somatic Emotional Release (SER) is a CranioSacral hands-on technique, named and developed by John Upledger, DO, which is used to rid the mind and body of residual effects of past injuries and negative experiences locked in body tissue. Practitioners can bypass the conscious mind and access the subconscious where suppressed emotions may remain recorded. Through autosuggestion, visualization, and symbolism one can reach a state of emotional awareness that facilitates a release of energies that can promote and create balance for inner healing.

An SER session is profoundly relaxing, so relaxing that a practitioner can assist the client to access the non-conscious to remember situations and emotions associated with the problem. The therapist, through dialoguing techniques and light touch with hands on the affected area, encourages the part of the mind that seeks to release the energy cysts (the problem). Often, the body assumes positions it was in when the accident or injury occurred and the patient will re-experience the emotions present at the time of the original incident. Once these suppressed experiences break through the surface, the problems can be dealt with and inner healing results."

After a short rest I worked on Jeanne by simply administering reflexology and the laying- on-hands on her troubled back. When I placed my hands on her back my hands began vibrating. I sensed that I didn't have enough energy to counteract her energy. I asked a gentleman by the name of Bob to come help me. Together we laid our hands on her and her back responded and cooled. (Later Jeanne informed me that she had back trouble often that took weeks to clear up. This time her pain left within a few days. +?)

Afterwards, as the group sat and chatted I learned more about each of their techniques and their lives. Bob told me he had been using healing touch on his farm animals for years. When he heard of this group he had joined them to experience using his gift with humans. I discovered Jeanne had been involved for several years in various different kinds of healing in St. Louis and had recently moved to Columbia. All had interesting stories.

I returned home with new books to read. I found the book *MAP- Medical Assistance Program* very informative that was written by Michelle Small Wright. The author describes the interesting theory of a spiritual medical team. She says this large group of highly evolved spirit souls are dedicated to assisting the evolutionary process of mankind - physically, emotionally, mentally and spiritually. Her book described my electrical jolts and some of my mysterious mystical experiences. I found some discrepancy with her theory because of the precise way she said one had to ask for help. I've been a recipient of these electrical jolts for some time without asking. I've been calling these happenings gifts of grace. I was indeed interested and intrigued. (I'd had assistance for a lengthy time. Now was this a name to place with it?) If there was such a team I prayed they would help me.

That night, during my sleep, hearing my name softly being called awakened me. + I opened my eyes and realized I was in bed. I then had an unusual experience. I heard, "Are you ready?" Then I literally felt hands moving across my body. At first I was afraid. I prayed, and then I relaxed. I wondered if the medical team MAP was at work. I saw lots of light with my eyes closed and wondered if I was going to remember the incident in the grass. I was awake for a long time and felt I was in the hands of power.

The next morning I kept feeling the urge to read Psalm 23. I wondered, "Why, Psalm 23?" As I read the Psalm of the Good Shepherd its meaning began to resonate deeply within me.

Yahweh is my shepherd, I lack nothing.

In the meadows of the green grass he lets me lie.

I began to tremble. I realized, without a doubt, that the ear message the day before had been God speaking to me. Jeanne was feeling the power of God in my right ear. God was communicating with me through her. I had felt the power and flame of His love. I recalled my earlier visions of the blessing of my right ear and the dove flying around my ear.

To the waters of repose he leads me; there he revives my soul.

The experience of CranioSacral was the most restful experience I'd ever encountered. I had truly felt I was resting with God.

He guides me by paths of virtue for the sake of his name.

I thought of my God messages, visions and dreams.

Though I pass through a gloomy valley, I fear no harm; beside me your rod and your staff are there, to hearten me.

I know I feel God's presence. I know He leads me in all I do.

You prepare a table before me under the eyes of my enemies; you anoint my head with oil, my cup brims over.

I vividly remembered my vision of drops of liquid being

Heavenly Text
inserted in a tube. Was what I witnessed the tube of my ear?
Ah, how goodness and kindness pursue me, every day of my life; my
home, the house of Yahweh, as long as I live.

I prayed: "God, I'm bowled over with gratitude. You
never cease to amaze me. Thank You for Your gift of
assurance on CranioSacral Therapy. I now understand that you
were letting me know that you are the breath of life, alive in
our bodies in the CranioSacral pulse that we each possess. You
have proved to me that this power, this energy is you. You
gave me more proof that my ear is a phone line to you. Were
the hands I felt moving over my body during the night the
medical assistance team? Have you been taking care of me in
this way without my knowledge and are now sharing this
information so I better understand? I know you are telling me
to not be afraid and that I must be prepared for whatever comes
my way in the future. I know you are with me. Thank you for
opening my ear in many ways. This was a powerful spiritual
experience. I realize this all happened on the 13th. Thank you.
Thank you. I love you. I'm overwhelmed with gratitude.
Keep leading me as you see fit."

I immediately called Jeanne explaining to her what
information I had just received. We chatted for some time and
then decided on another time to get together. I thanked God
that I had indeed found a new friend and teacher. I knew that
Jeanne's twenty years of experience in various healing
techniques, plus being a teacher of meditation, would all prove
to be invaluable.

When we got together we spent a couple of marvelous
hours sharing personal stories. I left with another stack of
books. She totally understands + and shared some of her own
mystical experiences. Jeanne told me that several years before,
Mother Mary had appeared briefly to her while she was
praying the rosary. She became teary-eyed as she explained,
"A friend of mine was in a terrible accident. I was fervently
praying for his life when I became aware of Mary standing a

165

couple of feet in front of me, with arms extended slightly from her sides. Unconditional love was pouring out of her arms and hands so strongly I felt it as a physical substance landing on me even as I was surrounded by it, much like a warm bath. The moment was brief but the message was clear: Everything would be O.K."

Jeanne also shared that she had been to Medjugorje and had a profound encounter on Apparition Hill. She said she was not expecting or asking to see anything special. At that time her life was full of turmoil and sadness and she was praying only for the gift of joy. However, her traveling companion was given an extraordinary gift. Her friend saw the spirit of Mary passing among the gathered spectators on Apparition Hill. As Mary passed through the crowd, she saw Mary lower her face and touch Jeanne's forehead.

July 22, 1995. I received a phone call at 7:45am from Eileen, the woman from the prayer group in Illinois. She told me that she now knew who it was that put us in touch with each other. She had been confused because she knew Sylvie by her married name, and I had used her maiden name. Her daughter, Pascale, had just been diagnosed with leukemia. My heart ached and I instantly knew I needed to be with them. I thanked Eileen for the information. All I could think of was another circle. How each of these women had sent me to the other in an unusual way. +

A few hours later I walked into the hospital room. Sylvie immediately said through tears, "I knew you would come. I knew you would. Thank heavens. I've been trying to call you and your name is not in the phone book. How did you know?" (The error of accidentally not being listed in the phone book that year caused multiple problems in our lives.)

Sylvie explained that Pascale, eighteen months old, had been diagnosed two days earlier and was already receiving chemotherapy. We shared tears and I offered my support and comfort. I was reliving those first moments of sorrow that I had experienced thirteen years before. We prayed together. I laid hands on Pascale. Sylvie was already using her chiropractic and acupuncture techniques.

Sylvie called a couple of days later and said she was awakened in the middle of the night. She saw a bright light and had an interior knowing that Pascale was going to be part of my book. I invited Sylvie to bring Pascale to our prayer group. Sylvie also shared a fascinating book with me, *The Essiac Report*, which is a tea that claimes cure for cancer and other diseases. This herb tea originates in Canada, which is Sylvie's homeland.

Essiac Report is about a nurse, Rene Caisse, who in 1922 was the head nurse at the Sisters of Providence Hospital in Ontario, Canada. Rene learned from a cured female patient a remedy for cancer, an herbal tea. The recipe was given to her by an Ojibwa Indian medicine man. The Indian had shared his tea because he understood the blessings of God are for all. He said, "This is a holy drink that will purify the body and place the body back in balance with the Great Spirit." (I believe this might have been +)

Rene understood that this tea was a detoxifier, which could free the body to heal from within. Two years later when Rene's aunt had liver and stomach cancer she administered this tea to her aunt with amazing results. The aunt lived twenty additional years. Rene then began brewing the tea and giving it to other terminally ill patients. She continued to have amazing success but was told to stop administering medicine without a license even though she was giving and not selling the tea.

Word spread and interest mounted but the medical authorities were less than impressed. Eventually she joined forces with Dr. Charles Brusch, a famous American doctor, who was the personal physician of former President John F. Kennedy. When Dr. Brusch was diagnosed with cancer, he tested the herbal tea on himself, without any additional medicine, and was completely cured of cancer. He joined the difficult process of getting it released to the public. Later Elaine Alexander joined them in trying to help obtain a way to spread the product here in the United States. Fighting a complicated system of Federal Drug Laws, testing, drug companies, etc., it became evident that it was best to market the tea through Health Food stores. Finally, the Flora Herbal distributing company started marketing the product in 1993 under the brand name Flor-Essence. Rene died in 1978. Many letters of testimony of various cures such as Diabetes, Hypoglycemia, Multiple Sclerosis, Parkinson, Arthritis, Chronic Fatigue Syndrome, Ulcers, etc. are included in this report. I was very impressed and feel this could be the biggest + ever. I also understand that there are other herbal combinations that detox one's body but Essiac seems to work with the majority.

It was becoming easier to reach out to others with my hands. I was becoming more and more convinced that Jesus still used many individuals in many ways to continue His work. Jesus did not heal people to prove He was God but to prove the power of God is available to us all. Throughout His public life He showed that healings could be a normal way of life if we become one in Spirit with Him. Jesus called His healings works, rather than miracles. Why has it taken nearly 2000 years for mankind to figure this out? I feel God has truly shown His patience, as He has waited for mankind to finally begin to learn, to know, and to use this "major gift" in our daily lives.

We read in scripture that the disciples imitated Christ in the healing ministry and had amazing results. The disciples encouraged us to imitate them as they were imitating Christ. Somewhere along the way, either by thinking ourselves unworthy, being told differently, or by not believing enough, we stopped readily using this gift.

I contend that this time in history God is prompting and urging us to grow into a new awareness of Spirit/energy and healing. God is pushing me to share and explain how I'm reinforcing my thoughts and beliefs. Healings are sometimes grouped with words such as occult, esoteric, new age, or spiritual. I intend to refute this assumption as I continue to blend the sacred with the secular. Mystics for over 5000 years have not spoken of energy fields, but their practices are consistent with what scientists are now discovering.

Newton (in 1729) was one of the first who began speaking of energy as light, as electrometric, as vibration. He felt God was present in nature through Spirit-light. The research work of Einstein in the early1900's made this knowledge become a fact of science. Since then many individuals have spent years researching electro dynamic fields in living organisms. It is now documented that this life flow of energy exists in humans, animals, plants, rocks, and the entire earth, the entire universe.

There have been over a 130 studies over recent years that have proven prayer improves the outcome of illness and leads to faster healing. Larry Dossey, M.D., has written two books (*Healing Words and Reinventing Medicine*) on this subject. He found that when he prayed with his patients, healings occurred faster than if he did not. He has conducted many studies to prove this.

There are many parallel views among modern physics, biology, psychology, science, eastern mysticism, and mystics on how energy affects the human body and mankind. We need to learn to embrace and combine all the information, thoughts, traditions, and ways of Spirit/energy in order to benefit from all its potentials. There have been many different opinions, expressions, and uses of Spirit/energy that have caused various differences and tensions over thousands of years, but it is possible to close the gap, to learn from differences. Over the centuries the strength in science has been rooted in actual experiences. The same will happen for medicine and religion. Time will make believers out of doubters. I feel Jesus is showing us that He is for us all by the very fact successful healings are being performed in many different religions, many different cultures, in many different ways, by many individuals that are not associated with organized religion. The scripture "They will lay-hands-on the sick, who will recover" (Matt 14:18) applies to everyone.

We need to be open and learn to distinguish fact from

Heavenly Text

fiction, science from fantasy, and knowledge from superstition. It is time for alternative-holistic- complementary healing to become mainstream. We are simply following in Jesus' footsteps when we become involved in healing.

I now understand how we are wired, with energy, just like a string of Christmas lights. When one part of us goes out the entire body feels it. Our bodies become unbalanced, we have pain, and disease sets in because our energy is out of sync. Because there are many ways to access this and restore this energy, many people have written books on "their" theory and way. But everyone is talking about the same Spirit/energy. There is no wrong way to reactivate a problem area by laying-on-of-hands. When one trusts his/her intuition by rubbing, pressing, pulling, massaging, simply using one's hands in a loving way phenomenal results can happen. Each of us has this limitless potential to extend to one another. Spirit/energy is available for all. I firmly believe that those who believe and reach out with their hands in love to help others heal physically, mentally or spiritually will sometimes have extraordinary results, which many call "miracles." I believe there are many successful ways to go about this: on a one-to-one basis, in groups, in churches, in homes. Didn't Jesus say, "Wherever two or more are together I am with you?" I believe reaching out in love with our hands to make others more comfortable is the purest form of love one can share with another. Our hands are supreme gifts. I know the power of compassionate touch is immense. I believe the power of touch used with knowledge of the energy system has the ability to enhance one's life in a physical way.

Society views the body as a physical machine that needs something tangible to make it well. Scientific technical gadgetry, drugs, and the like have too long swayed our society. With knowledge, experiences and time I am comfortable in saying **we "all" are born with the potential to heal one another and ourselves. We just have to find the belief and put it to use.** + It's called **TRUST**. + There is little room for excusing ourselves when we read Jesus words, "I tell you most solemnly, whoever believes in me will perform the same works as I do myself, he will perform even greater works, because I am going to the Father." (John 14:12)

I incorporate the techniques and methods that I've learned--all various methods of laying on of hands. Many individuals go to school for months and years to receive degrees in order to utilize these techniques, but for me the information has all been a gift from individuals sharing their gifts (knowledge and books). I'm convinced anyone can learn as I have. The gift is available to all.

I am now trying to instruct and teach others simple ways in which they can help their loved ones through touch and prayer. I do not feel healings have to take place in a Pentecostal service, charismatic atmosphere, or church, but can take place on a one-to-one basis in the home. I highly encourage parents to lay hands on their children when they are ill. I encourage everyone to reach out to anyone who is ill. Reaching out with loving hands one might be surprised at the instant results. And on the practical level this love could drastically reduce medical cost.

When administering and using my hands I have learned to quiet myself to feel a sense of peace. I unite my thoughts with God and ask for His Spirit to be present. I ask God to use me as a "vessel" of His power. I then proceed to simply lay my hands on the individual in troubled energy spots to share God's power. Sharing unconditional love helps bring peace to the soul and comfort to the individual. For me, all of this is working. I have found a complete integrated way to help my neighbor in another loving way. I feel comfortable in my new-found knowledge, and I know I will keep learning more. I am feeling empowered by God.

I pray: "Thank You God for my new found courage and knowledge. You fill my days with delight and joy. Because of the steady stream of information that has come into my life, I now better understand the ancient wisdom story on healing that you so lovingly shared with me. I pray you will be with others as they read my words so that they too can find the courage and

Heavenly Text
trust to reach out to others with loving hands. I love you. "

July 28, 1995. + I experienced a very clear vision of angels quickly moving, almost running, down a church aisle. There seemed to be at least a dozen. I thought the vision interesting but did not have a clue what it meant.

The next day I happened to read a book written by June Howard on learning how to commune with one's angel. When I read the last page I was startled when I read, "Imagine yourself seeing the angels that help you coming down a church aisle." + I had seen earlier in a vision the very thing that was being described here. I was dumbfounded. I reread more intently.

July 30, 1995. + I again had a vision of an eye crying tears. Many hurricanes were occurring at this time, and I presumed I was being told of another tragedy. I did not know the location. I believe I was being told to pray.

August 3, 1995. I returned to Helen's prayer house in Kentucky, this time with my good friend Jane. I awoke around 3am and as I thought about the day ahead I asked Mother Mary for a favor as I prayed, "You've often showered me with gifts, but I'd give anything if Jane could experience something special today at Helen's."

Around 9am Erv went to play golf with some of my brothers. Jane picked me up. We reached Helen's home in time for the 10am prayer session. There was a small group present. During the hour of prayers I was again amazed and astounded to see the spirit of Sister Faustina very clearly in the room. Not once but five times. + Chills abounded each time and I cried in gratitude wondering, "Why?" When the prayers were over Helen said, I have a message from Mary.

+*"My children, you are called to live as apostles in the middle of the world. You must get into the habit of speaking only to those who will comfort you in your faith. You must introduce people slowly to my love. You cannot operate always on your level. The only way to win apostles for me is to*

172

show them you understand where they are. You must go to their level of understanding. You cannot start talking of miracles if they don't know the basis of the faith or their belief will be shallow and more than that you will get a cold response. Be warm, be understanding, be gentle, be humble, be prudent, be calm, and remember no one can harm your soul. So I beg you to prayer. Visit my Son. Fast. Say the Rosary every day. I am your Heavenly Mother, Mary."

+ Wow! Did that hit home. Here I was on the way to a family gathering where some are totally unaware of my mystical experiences, and those who are aware remain voiceless or appear uninterested. I remembered the cold response I received the last time.

I heard Jane say, "I think that message was for me." The others in the room remarked that they didn't totally understand what the message meant. Helen explained, "Usually those whom the message is meant for are the ones who understand. I never know who the messages will be for. I just write them down as they are audibly dictated to me by Mary."

Obviously the message was for both of us. After the others departed Jane and I spent an hour talking with Helen and her husband, Jay. I asked Helen how she receives messages. She explained, "Often, I'm awakened in the middle of the night. I hear an audible clear voice that says, 'I have a message.' I get up and get a pen and paper. It takes me awhile to write the messages down. Mary is very patient and gentle and she talks to me slowly." I asked, "When did you receive this message?" Helen replied, "I was awakened last night about 3:15am."

+ Chills! I remembered my request at 3am. ("Thank you. Thank you, my Heavenly Mother." I vow to myself not to say anything, or push my ideas on anyone ever again unless asked.)

Jane and I spent the rest of the day together. We had written the message down and reread it several times. We shared many feelings and thoughts. I often think to myself that Elizabeth was for Mary like Jane is for me. God knows everyone needs support. I find it very difficult not to be able to share all that is happening in my life with everyone I see, especially my family. I get so excited. I guess that's why writing it all down is good. I know in my heart the day will come when others will read my story and welcome the chance to share in the experiences. I certainly understand the message from Jesus in scripture, "A prophet is only despised in his own country, among his own relatives and in his own house." (Mark 6:4)

August 10, 1995. This was the evening my friend Sylvie brought her daughter Pascale to our prayer group. After Mass Fr. Mike anointed Pascale and all present laid hands on her as prayers of healing were prayed. Bless her heart, Pascale broke out in a sweat and began to cry. There was a tremendous amount of Spirit/energy for one little girl. Only time would tell if our prayers were answered.

August 16, 1995. I received a phone call from Sylvie. She was full of joy and enthusiasm. The bone marrow on this day, the first since our prayers, showed no cancer cells. Pascale was in remission. Sylvie was elated. ("Thank you, thank you, thank you, God. Even though the doctors want to continue a lesser degree of on-going chemotherapy for awhile I feel you definitely answered our prayers.") But sadly, five years later, Pascale's leukemia did return (I often wondered if the chemo had weakened her causing the cancer to return), that ultimately resulted in a bone marrow transplant. Today (2010) Pascale is doing well.

August 17, 1995. I went back to Jeanne's for more Spirit/energy work and CranioSacral therapy. At least this time I thought I knew what to expect. But when Jeanne scanned my body for disturbed energy spots she zeroed in on my lungs, telling me she felt the lung problem was from a past life. In my mind I questioned, "Past life? Do I believe in reincarnation? I know the church doesn't believe in reincarnation. But I had to admit I have often thought that if a soul would get a chance to come back to earth, over and over, it would eventually work things out and get to heaven. I know as a mother I couldn't punish my child by condemning them, but I could certainly give them another chance. I like to think that's how God thinks. Who knows for sure? I'll just go along with the process here and see what happens." (More later on how I now believe in reincarnation. It has been proven to me.) Jeanne then began to tell me she was visualizing a monk. That she thought I had died from a terrible lung disease. I had come back to this life not consciously remembering, but my subconscious remembered. I instantly remembered the doctor saying that I was born with my foot problem. Jeanne then went to the spot on my foot (the lung meridian) that occasionally still gave me some discomfort and began applying pressure, pressure like Anne had used in the past. An amazing thing happened. My foot vibrated, relaxed, and I felt energy escaping from it. + This went on for some time. It was similar to the energy release that I had when Anne worked on my foot. Jeanne explained to me that this was what somatic emotional release was all about. A therapist, through dialogue techniques encourages part of the mind to release the energy cyst in the body in order for the individual to heal from within. One can take the remarks either literally or metaphorically, but there is usually therapeutic benefit.

This was all truly amazing and still bizarre to me but I actually felt more pressure relief in my foot. I decided to not worry about the past life part, pretend it's all just a story, a symbolism, whatever, because the results were good. I came home elated. What a unique experience it had been.

Jeanne recommended I start practicing Yoga to help me breathe deeper and help strengthen my lungs. She came over to my house a few days later and showed me a routine of Yoga positions. Jeanne explained that Yoga emerges from traditions that date back to 1000 B C. The word Yoga means union or communion with God. The purpose of Yoga is to balance the mind, body and spirit with the universe - with God. Yoga also promotes fitness, grace, flexibility, relaxation; it steadies the mind, calms emotions, and tones the body. The practice of

Heavenly Text

Yoga is commonplace in some Eastern religions. Yoga also enhances one's health because of deep breathing and stretching. Deep breathing gives the body more oxygen, nourishes the muscles and invigorates the mind. If done properly, Yoga is a way to get the breath of life into every cell. Through inner awareness one can also come in touch with one's soul-self and access a higher consciousness.

I was stiff and could hardly do any of the positions correctly, but I was determined. I began doing Yoga daily. I was finally doing what I had been introduced to in my readings in Gulf Shores.

August 19, 1995. + I had a vision of seeing a group of nuns. I wondered if it was Sister Faustina, but I could not clearly see the style of their habits. I laughingly thought to myself, "Jeanne said I was once a monk, not a nun. Why this?"

August 20, 1995. + I was awakened with another electrical shock. Since these often precede gifts, I gave thanks not knowing what gift was in store.

Later that day I read a very interesting article in a magazine on a person named Maitreya. This was the first time I've ever heard this name. The author, a Buddhist, explained that he thought Meitreya was Jesus reincarnated and already here on earth to guide and lead us into a new era. It fascinates me how all faiths express their beliefs in different ways. All religions have their own stories of how Christ will reappear. I figured the more I open myself to reading the more I'll eventually be able to better discuss the subject more universally because I definitely know each culture's views are different.

August 25, 1995. Anne arrived again for a few days for more lessons and appointments. The first evening I had arranged an informational meeting for her to speak on holistic medicine. Interest was piqued among those present- about thirty. I was excited that the circle of individuals interested in alternative/holistic medicine was expanding.

A workshop on body reflexology was scheduled for the next day. Re-learning the pressure points that run throughout our body was very enlightening. It enhanced my understanding of the connection of these invisible rivers of energy meridians.

August 28, 1995. I woke during the night to a profound happening. I felt like a bucket of water was being poured over my head. + It reminded me of my electrical shocks but different. It actually felt like water. I wasn't wet so I called it a "bucket of energy." + I believe God's helpers gave me a high dose of energy because a lot was going to be happening in the near future.

That very afternoon Anne did reflexology on my feet. She found tender spots that told her something was going on with my kidneys. She moved her hands to the pressure points on my legs that are on the meridian line of the kidneys. I felt pain at the pressure points, then a sudden headache. Anne started repeating, "Breathe, breathe, breathe deeply." And bingo, all of a sudden I had the strangest sensation. I felt a movement of energy enter at my left foot and felt it travel up my left side, up through my head, and down my right side and out my right foot. My hands began to tingle and my headache left. I exclaimed, "I got it. I just felt the meridian opening. I got it! I got it! + God has finally gotten the message through to this thick skull about what you've been telling me. I felt the energy surge, opening and pulsating throughout my body." My hands were tingling like crazy and Anne suggested putting them in saltwater. And more amazement: I saw bubbles rising to the surface of the water radiating from my hand. I quizzically asked, "Why my kidney?" Anne explained to me again about body memory. "Your body still had that memory pain from all your kidney problems. That meridian has been closed for years, probably all your life since you were born with a deformed kidney. Your meridian is now open. Your body is healing from within." (In 1960 doctors discovered I had a deformed kidney and I had surgery to remove it.) I wondered and asked, "Why suddenly now?" She explained, "We don't know why. But your body knows when and how to heal itself when one co-operates." I asked, "Could this happening have anything to do with my Yoga. " Anne agreed and said, "By doing Yoga you're helping your body to wake up. Yoga also means union with God." I was remembering the ancient wisdom lesson that told me healing is like a streak of lightning coming up from the earth, going through the person and exiting back to the earth.

I was filled with amazement. I felt I understood what I had been reading about but experiencing it made it more profound and memorable. I had felt the energy flow at Jeanne's, and now here is this energy felt so clearly. My body was self-correcting in many places. What a gift! I was surprised and elated. (I exclaimed, "So that's why my bucket of energy this morning. Thanks, God.")

August 31, 1995. I went to see Jeanne again and she began administering somatic emotional release techniques. As she placed her hands on my lung, she told me she thought I had TB in one of my lifetimes. I thought, "Here we go again with this past life memory stuff." All I could think of was, "No wonder my foot was born deformed with all of this lung memory she keeps bringing up - multiple lung problems." She then proceeded to work on my left foot again and the craziest thing started happening with the corresponding fingers on my left hand. My middle fingers began to tighten up and pull forward without my moving them. When I realized the fingers were in the same meridian as my toes, I thought, "Here we go again." Jeanne exclaimed, "I feel bones moving, ligaments moving here in your foot." As she applied pressure to my foot and toes, surges of energy power went through my leg, up my trunk, down my arm, through my fingers. Bingo! Another meridian opened. I was again dumbfounded. Elated. Mystified. Thrilled. + I could hardly believe it. I knew that I had just felt another energy surge. Jeanne remarked, "You're really opening the lines of air to your body. Your body seems to be healing within in many places."

I knew that I'd been faithful with trying to breath deeper in meditation and in doing my Yoga. I had twisted and turned more than ever before in my life. Powerful thoughts and feelings kept tumbling around in my mind. ("Thanks, God. What a gift. I don't have the words in my vocabulary to expound on this, but you know how I feel in my heart.")

September 3, 1995. + I had a very profound dream. I was made aware that when the truth is spoken in working with someone in healing, sometimes pictures and visions result. My dream gave me clarification of what I had been experiencing. I heard, "*Facilitators have visions and tell stories to walk one through to an understanding of their problem so healing can begin within for that person.*" I rejoiced knowing that God sends messages in multiple ways. I recalled the prophesy from the Iowa prayer group and from others administering Spirit/energy work on me.

September 4, 1995. I had a fascinating dream in which I was taught the understanding and importance of keener awareness. + Since it was an awareness I'm at a loss in how to explain what was relayed to me. There just aren't words.

I told God, "If nothing else, I really needed 'the bucket of energy' to muster the courage to write about these extraordinary events. The powerful information you've been leading me through these last days is overwhelming and I realize might be confronting for others. Thanks for the healings."

September 6, 1995. I went to see Jeanne again. This time my left shoulder seemed to be demanding the attention. I heard a story from Jeanne about being left behind in England in the 1600's that resulted in making me afraid, fearful of being alone. At that time I had withdrawn and it showed in my posture. Again there was release of energy but nothing as dramatic as before. I felt it in my shoulder area. Jeanne named a day for us to get together again the next week. When I wrote the date she suggested on my calendar I realized the date was the 13th. I could hardly wait.

September 7, 1995. + I had a vision of a hurricane doing excessive damage. I prayed for those in its path.

In the morning after my bath I suddenly experienced tremendous pressure in my head. I had to lie down. Then in my mind's eye I began to see a bright Light, like the sun. The living eye appeared in the middle of this bright Light and then inside of this Light I saw Anne working on me. (Fascinating. I could hardly wait to tell her. "Thanks, God.")

September 9, 1995. + I was awakened by a strong electrical jolt. Then I felt I was in the hands of the unknown. As strange as it sounds I think I had another body alignment from within. I was receiving help from an unknown source. I know I was not moving any part of my body on my own. I felt my body reflexing, moving, and responding not to me but to something else. At one point I literally felt the heel of my foot completely rotate. There was a gentle pain with the movement. It felt like my ankle changed positions. I keep remembering the "bucket of energy" as my healing from within continued. +

I prayed, "I'm getting the message, God, loud and clear. Your healing power never ceases to amaze me. How am I ever going to be able to explain all of this? I know you'll help me. Thank you, Thank you."

September 13, 1995. I arrived at Jeanne's for another treatment. I asked, "Do my shoulders look lop-sided to you? It sure feels lop-sided to me. Ever since you worked on my shoulders I haven't felt like me. My right shoulder is higher." Jeanne agreed she could see the difference. After balancing and relaxing my energies, she started applying pressure on my right shoulder. There was a tremendous energy release and then the strangest thing: my arm started rotating in a strange way. It felt like an invisible person was holding my arm as it proceeded to rise into the air. My arm nudged gradually, a half an inch at a time, into a complete circular rotation that must have taken thirty minutes to an hour. Jeanne asked, "Have you ever been around a Murphy bed?" "When we were kids we lived at my grandmother's house and there were two beds in the wall in the sunroom," I responded. Jeanne remarked, "I think this problem resulted from a bed like that--that's the vision I'm getting," My body chilled and reacted to that statement as if it were true. + I remembered how as youngsters we use to hide behind the bed while playing hide and seek. I answered, "Maybe I got stuck once and dislodged something. Who knows? I don't remember ever sleeping there, but maybe I did." As she continued to apply pressure, my arm kept rotating, and we felt muscles jumping, bones moving and experienced more energy being released. It was another unexplainable occurrence. Since the date was the 13th of September I was thanking and giving credit to my heavenly Mother Mary for this experience on her day. +

September 15, 1995. + I spent another night of being awakened to more bodywork and alignment from an unknown source. When I fell back asleep an unusual dream on healing occurred. I was helping a lady stranger who was in pain. When I awoke I had a vision. + Hands with palms up were being crossed with a beam of Light. This repeated several times. It was a strange awareness, but I knew I was seeing my hands being blessed or prepared for something. This crossing type of ceremony repeated itself several times. ("Thanks God, I'm overwhelmed.")

September 24, 1995. + I had a vision of being above my body and seeing Erv and myself in our bed. I could see Jesus beside our bed giving a blessing. I saw Jesus making various blessing gestures over me.

I prayed, "Thanks Jesus, I need all you can give me. This stuff you have me writing is strange and more and more difficult to explain. I know my body had been changed a great deal. I can bend my arms back like never before and my shoulders have taken on a major change in appearance. I can also do arm positions in Yoga I couldn't do before. This realignment work these past weeks is nothing short of amazing. Thanks for your love, your help, and the bucket of energy." (Anne called the next day to tell me she was returning.)

I think for too long we have been ignorant of our body's potential. I know I was. Most of us have been reaching to others to solve our problems when instead we can help ourselves more than we ever dreamed. I now know our bodies process the power to heal from within. My soul had been enlightened and enhanced by another inner awareness - His breath of life that dwells within us all. I had found that I could plug into this subtle power of God, this Spirit/energy, not only for my spiritual well-being but my physical well-being. I had learned through personal experience that meditation and Yoga are a connection with Spirit that can be used for spiritual and physical nourishment.

To mediate and practice Yoga is so simple that many in our culture don't give them value. I had found through Yoga and meditation that breathing directs my awareness and energy to different body parts for enhanced concentration and relaxation. Sadly, meditation and Yoga are rarely, if ever, taught in any church. I now knew how important it is that a disciplined life of prayer and meditation should be coupled with church attendance. I don't mean simple contemplation or passive meditation, but a deep active level of meditation with controlled breathing that can increase our creativity and help our health. For too long churches have been willing to accept the status quo of intellectual faith without truly believing that each of us is called to experience union with God. Not enough emphasis is given to the verse: "The nearer you go to God, the nearer He will come to you." (James 4:8)

I should have realized sooner to put more emphasis on my breath as a connection to God. "Then He breathed into his nostrils a breath of life, and thus man became a living being,

Heavenly Text
(Genesis 2:3) is certainly something I've heard often but I didn't totally understand. Now I do.

Yoga and mediation had become a way of life for me that changed my inner awareness and awakened my physical mind and body. I was amazed at how much my body responded in such a short time. I know my health improved and meditation brought my mind from the surface of life to the depth of my being. Meditation has become like a phone-line to God, where I encounter the subtle energies of the universe. I have found divine guidance comes from peace and quiet and asking for it. CranioSacral Therapy introduced me to a deeper relaxation and helped me find a depth of awareness that I did not know existed. Then I learned to reach this deep awareness with meditation. It took time for me to learn to be quiet enough, still enough, believing enough, to open these channels to heaven.

Meditation is not an escape from reality, but discovering and becoming in touch with a new reality. Meditation can help one find one's self. It makes our unused self come into being. To truly know God we must be open and present. I now better understand the quote, "Pause awhile and know that I am God." (Psalm 46:10) By using meditation as a way of learning about ourselves, we can come to understand mind over matter.

God had been healing my body--pruning it like a tree. I now understood that- emotional remembering is the communication link between the brain, the immune system, and our emotions. When we become balanced and in harmony, amazing changes take place. I'd experienced this healing within. I think this knowledge, these healings, will become commonplace for all in the near future. I believe because I know, because it has happened to me.

September 29, 1995. + A different type of vision. I saw the eye, it kept getting larger and larger. Then I seemed to be going into the pupil of the eye. It felt like I went through the eye. In the distance I saw Jesus, on His knees, in the desert praying fervently. The scene was brief but distinct.

183

Heavenly Text

I've read in Scripture that Jesus went into the desert to rest. He was human and He, too, needed days to resolve conflicts in His mind, to touch base with His Father, to rekindle His own Spirit, to heal Himself. I wondered if this was the message He was sharing with me.

When I visited Fr. Mike and shared my thoughts he said, "Your writings bring to mind the Scripture from Ecclesiastes 38."

October 10, 1995. + I again saw Jesus' exposed Sacred Heart and various scenes in the life of Christ: Christ carrying a cross on His shoulder; Christ hanging on the cross; Christ administering healing to individuals. I felt my teacher was sharing with me that in doing healing work I would be sharing in His sufferings. I cried with gratitude. I knew I had a Divine teacher.

October 12, 1995. Our prayer group was overwhelmed with joy when we received a personal message from Mother Mary through one of our members. The message took us all by surprise. I again thought of the women in Iowa. This gift of prophecy is spellbinding when it happens. Several times we've had messages from Jesus but this was our prayer group's first message from Mary and there was a different feeling of presence in the room.

+"*My daughters, my Son has sent me to you today. I am your Mother Mary. (I wiped away tears as I listened in awe to the personal message to our group.) Your prayers are pleasing to Jesus, especially your prayers of thanksgiving and prayers for others. Your prayers have been heard and are answered. They rise up to My Son like a sweet fragrance. We appreciate your discipline and what you do for others. The charity you do for others is an example for others as my Son's life and my life were examples. Be at peace and love one another.* "

In discussion afterwards, we learned from the person speaking that she had had a mental vision of Mary as she relayed what she heard. She told us she saw Mary dressed in white, surrounded in gold glitter, standing on a bed of roses. We felt honored, and we prayed in appreciation. I thought of my vision two days previous. It was exactly one year ago, on October 13, 1994, that our prayer group had formed. What a wonderful anniversary gift.

October 13, 1995. Scheduling made it impossible for all the prayer group members to go, but Elaine and I returned to Our Lady of Snows. We arrived early, and I was fortunate to again visit with Ray before the apparition. I was saddened to learn that his wife had died on July 13. I remarked as I hugged him, "Certainly you know God took her on His Mother's special day to make it clear to you June has gone home to heaven?" He nodded his knowing. We visited for a while and agreed to a future meeting.

Later, after Mary appeared to Ray, he read the message he had received. He began by saying, "Today Mary was dressed differently then usual, she was in white and gold." + Elaine and I both felt in our hearts confirmation of our visit the night before. The message was lengthy. My heart ached to hear at one point, "The Chastisement has begun." Already I knew this to be true because of all the natural disasters and worldly tragic occurrences that had abounded in recent months. It was another reminder that I still needed to write more on that subject.

October 21, 1995. Anne arrived for more classes, this time a seminar for nurses. Erv and I went to the University of Missouri's football game while she gave her seminar. Late that afternoon, we had all returned and were visiting in our family room when I noticed my right eye was acting strangely. I was losing clarity in my vision. When I shut my eyes I saw strange geometric patterns. I experienced the strange sensations for several minutes before I said anything. I announced, "My eyes are acting somewhat like I remember years ago when I would get migraine headaches." I then got up and went to the restroom. I experienced shooting pains in my bladder as I urinated. I thought to myself, "This is not good. Something very strange is happening here." I returned to the room and asked Anne, "Are the kidney and bladder meridians connected?" She immediately answered, "You know they are. What is going on with you?" I explained in depth my unusual symptoms. She looked into my eyes and suggested she work on me.

We went to the bedroom and I lay on the bed as she began checking the kidney meridian on my right foot. It was very sensitive and painful. She said, "Breathe deeply. We're going to try to release some toxins from your kidney." As she applied pressure I felt pain not only in my foot but in my right side radiating toward my bladder. Shortly, the pain released and we discussed the problem. Anne asked, "Have you had much liquid today?" I had to admit I hadn't. She suggested I drink some hot water immediately and then start drinking cranberry juice and/or eat parsley.

We returned to the family room and as I drank the liquid I noticed shortly thereafter my right eye began to clear but my left eye started getting fuzzy. Anne explained the left eye was probably acting this way in sympathy and was trying to bring about balance. Sure enough in a few minutes my vision was back to normal. As we discussed all of the unusual symptoms, she explained that I had just experienced a silent migraine. Something I'd never heard of. She suggested I needed to take special care not to let toxins build in my kidney again and to always drink plenty of fluids. "You know you have a weakness there. You're lucky you've become so sensitive that you recognize warning signals," she said.

I vowed to take her advice and knew I would pay closer attention not to abuse my one kidney. Then she briefly explained iridology and how much information comes from the eye. She explained how the iris of our eyes is like a miniature TV set of the remote areas of our body. The iris reveals our strengths and weaknesses, what is correct and incorrect in our bodies. The iris of the eye is connected to every organ and tissue in the body by way of the brain and nervous system. The iris' greatest asset is the ability to forewarn of approaching difficulties before symptoms occur by revealing toxic settlement and accumulation. I marveled at how my body had given me the warning. I was further impressed with Anne's knowledge and how she continues to teach me so much.

I confided, "I don't think God is expecting me to learn and do all you do. I think He wants me to learn so I can write about how our bodies heal from within but I think my calling is simply to have faith, to know that He can use me as a vessel of healing for myself and for others. I continually feel more and more comfortable in simply laying hands on others in order to share energy. I don't feel a need to manipulate areas. I have faith in God. I believe the angels do the work. I believe in miracles. I trust He'll take care of what needs to be done."

Anne responded with, "I agree that is best, and I've witnessed many miracles, but I think many individuals need to talk and to experience manipulation in order to figure out the real powers of healing. What I have done for years is to help people relearn the truth about themselves. Mankind as a whole has' forgotten who they are, where they came from, what their purpose is. Once people get a handle on how their emotions effect their own illness and regain their faith in themselves and in God, they begin to remember and they then begin to heal."

I continued, "For several years I've been growing and healing spiritually and then you came along and helped me to understand how to participate in my own physical healing. I'm so impressed how you give and give of yourself and have trained multitudes."

As we continued to talk and share from our hearts I thanked God over and over for the gifts of His power, for the gift of Anne in my life, for the joy of His mysteries, for the gift of His love and knowledge.

October 23, 1995. When I got out of bed I could hardly walk. I had the strangest pain on top of my left foot, something I'd never felt before. I limped into the kitchen complaining to Anne, "You seem to bring out the worst in me. Whenever I'm around you these crazy things happen to me. I don't know whether to blame you or God. Although I do think He just wants me to learn more from you. What could this be?" She commented, "Experience is the best teacher." Immediately she went to work on my foot. "It's your thymus. Your immune system is in need of some strengthening." I wondered if this had anything to do with the kidney problem two days before. Anne agreed and explained to me that anytime our bodies slough off or take on anything it affects all of our body in many different ways. She explained how stirring up the immune system could be good and cleansing. She proceeded to demonstrate how to effectively remove pain and discomfort by using her body as a conduit to release the pain. I was amazed at the amount of heat that radiated from me through her hand. + My foot immediately improved. Amazing!

October 27, 1995. Before Anne left she worked on me again. This time she concentrated on my head. She gently placed her hands on my head to relax me. Shortly she exclaimed, "Do you hear that singing?" I replied in the negative. She said, "I keep hearing monks singing--Tibetan monks chanting." I thought, "Here goes that monk thing again." She also shared that she was having sensations that made her aware that I had had severe lung trouble. I then shared my experiences that I'd had with Jeanne. Shortly my body began to quiver and shake from the hips down. This lasted several minutes. I had no control over it. Then she placed her hands on my face. I asked, "Are you moving your hands?" She answered, "They're as still as can be." I replied, "Amazing. Not to me. It feels like your hands are moving. I feel a circular sensation deep in my head." + All I could jokingly think to say was, "I guess my tired brain needs a massage."

When we finished I shook my head, exclaiming, "Anne, I'll never figure all of this strange stuff out but it sure is interesting and seems to be working. I'm learning. I've now experienced God healing me through others' loving touch from head to toe. It's just all so amazing." She replied, "Isn't life fun? God makes it all so interesting."

I again thanked God and confided, "I understand more and more the scripture quote, 'whoever keeps His commandments lives in God and God lives in Him.' (1John 3:24) I feel the Spirit throughout my body as I've continued to heal. I wonder what exciting things you have in store for me next. I now understand what progressive healing is all about. Thank you so much."

October 28, 1995. + A vision in the middle of the night. I again saw an eye crying tears.

October 29, 1995. + A very strange and puzzling vision. I saw several scenes of people in normal circumstances such as on a street, out in a field, sitting on rocks. Each time there was a scene I'd see a bright spark of Light appear on the person's body. The spark would grow rapidly in size, and then the individual would disappear in a flash. I saw maybe a half a dozen people who seemed to get zapped by this Light and vanish.

It was a powerful vision, yet confusing. I didn't have a clue what was going on. Lots of questioning thoughts went through my mind: Am I witnessing healings or miracles? Am I seeing people get killed or saved? Are these new levels of seeing, new levels of believing? Am I witnessing vanishing in the twinkle of an eye? I prayed and asked God to show me more so I might better understand what I was viewing, but no other visions appeared.

November 10/11, 1995. I went to Topeka, Kansas, with a friend to attend the traveling show of the Treasures of the Czars. It was the most significant collection of royal and state treasures ever to leave the Moscow Kremlin Museum. It was extremely interesting and I was amazed at the opulence and extravagance of the Romanovs. The exhibition revealed that old Russia believed God manifested Himself through artistic expression. To see the immense size of the stones, jewels, and pearls that decorated the church vestments, chalices, tabernacles, patens, etc., was a stark contrast to the Russia I've heard about in my lifetime. It became evident to me that the church was more concerned with image then with the people, thus the collapse of religion in Russia. No wonder Mother Mary asked at Fatima that Russia be converted. It had gone from one extreme to another. Hopefully all religions will take note.

That evening I spent the night with my teacher friend Di, who is now teaching in the Topeka school system. The next morning God involved me in a profound healing experience. Tia, Di's daughter, was recovering from surgery on her upper arm. She had had some bone grafting done due to improper healing of the area. She had previously had a growth removed that did not heal properly. Tia's arm was now in a cast.

In the early morning when Tia came downstairs she sat on the couch and exclaimed, "My hand is swollen this morning." I heard a distinct inner voice say, "Nancy, Go help Tia." + I instinctively got up, went to her side, lifted her arm and placed it on my shoulder as I placed my hands around her upper arm cast. The heat was intense. She immediately asked, "What is that I'm feeling? It feels like motion going on in my arm." I shared with her that I was also feeling the movement. "Mom, come feel this," she called out. Di attempted to feel the pulsation that was very intense to Tia and me. After a couple of minutes I literally felt an electrical shock + which caused me to jump, my hand to react, and Tia yelled out, "What was that?" I began to try to explain, meridians, energy sensations, and healing from within. Tia said, "I don't know what just happened but my feet were cold, my arm was hot, and it felt like electricity." I assured her she was very sensitive and that's why she had felt what she did. I explained that she had felt the power of God. I shared that I had a similar experience a few weeks prior. I encouraged Di to lay her hands on her daughter every day. I knew in my heart that this time Tia would heal properly.

Heavenly Text

November 22, 1995. + I had a long vision of the eye beaming Light towards me. This happened over and over. I felt His warmth and love.

November 24, 1995. During a sleepless night I was praying and asking God, "How can I become even closer to You?" I began to see the eye with a small beam of Light radiating towards me. Then suddenly the eye tilted and a huge wide beam radiated outward. + The beam got broader and wider until I seemed to be engulfed in entire Light.

I thanked God and asked many questions. "Are you showering me with Light? Are you telling me I need to let more of your Light in? Are you giving me more Light? Are you telling me I need to give more Light out to others? I'm confused. Can you help me understand?" Time passed as I prayed. I kept hearing internally. +*"Try fasting more." "Try meditating more."* I promised God I'd try harder.

November 29, 1995. + I clearly saw many objects flying around, but I couldn't figure out what the objects were. The vision repeated itself again and again. It was confusing. Many objects that were blowing and other objects were floating in water.

I thought to myself, I hope Fr. Mike can figure this out. I sure can't.

December 1, 1995. I visited Fr. Mike and we discussed the past week's visions. He was also at a loss to the meaning of the last two visions but said, "I'm sure there is a good interpretation of these and we will know in time." We prayed for God to enlighten us to their meaning.

It didn't take long for that prayer to be answered. After our visit we both went to noon mass. I immediately knew the answer during the first reading. It was from Daniel, "In the first year of Belshazzar, Daniel had a dream and a vision that passed through his head as he laid in bed. He wrote the dream down, and this is how the narrative began: "I have been seeing

191

visions in the night. I saw four winds stirring up the sea"
(Daniel 7:1-2) + I knew in my heart that Daniel's vision was
similar to the vision God had shown me. I looked up at Fr.
Mike and he smiled. After Mass I said, "I think we got the
answer to one of my visions. In my heart I know it's time for
me to write what I've been putting off. I'm supposed to write
more on His Ultimate Power."

I prayed, "Please help me, God, as I go about a very hard
task. I know it's what you expect and want from me. I know
you will guide and enlighten me. Thank you for having faith in
me to do this."

The next day I began. All power, ultimate power is in the
hands of God. The power of God created life. The power of
God can heal, and the power of God can create. I believe God
is awakening mystical experiences and encounters with the
Divine in many places, to resurrect the human spirit and to
bring about an era with Christ as our head.

We individuals are a small part of creation just as birds,
animals, trees, the earth, and the universe are a part of the
whole. It appears to me that we've grown to become more
interested in ourselves and our individual desires than in the
understanding of what it means to be a small part of the
creation of God. It is imperative that the minds of the world
learn to work in cooperation with the mind of God because the
fate of all creation rests in our hands. I feel the world's attitude
must change, and change soon. It is time for all of us to think
in terms of our world as our neighborhood and treat it as such;
not to destroy but to rebuild, not to put down but to add to, not
to give up on but to join in.

We, all denominations of faith, can work together with
love, operating from our hearts to change the world and usher
in the Kingdom of God. I believe God is watching over us and
we are all participating in the birthing of new creation.
Whenever there is major change needed the power of God
seems to manifest itself more. This is what I feel is happening
now in our time - the end of this era. I think history will prove

this is the time of an awakening here on earth which will go down in Biblical history.

It seems the earth is trying to heal itself, by renewing itself often in a display of natural disasters. I feel we all need to come to the realization that these fundamental changes will, in the long run, enhance the life of all living things in our universe. Throughout all of spiritual history we have witnessed God's power and how suffering helped to create a greater good and greater awareness.

Jesus showed His power of turning bad into good many times. He demonstrated different types of power and suffering by His death on the cross and by His resurrection. We learn throughout the written word that those who follow Christ will share in His sufferings and His Glory. I feel each generation learns from the past. It seems to me that suffering is the natural result of spiritual disorder. Each generation manifests in a new way.

In the Book of Revelation John's written word warns us of God's power. John explains that an era of great sufferings, great pain, and great testing will come about at the end times, at the end of an era. John constructs a symbolic universe in order to make sense out of the Christian experience. John's words move from fear and promise to fulfillment.

At this time in history it is apparent that the world is in turmoil. As humans we are confused, and we project turmoil and uncertainty around us. It seems to me the positive forces of life like freedom, bliss, and enjoyment, have all been lost to fear and tension. The collective consciousness of all human's behavior is destroying our earth. The earth mirrors our behavior. Tension in life creates tension in nature. Man has wandered from God's plan and has substituted materialism, violence, and greed. Too many have forgotten that God is our leader. The Divine Plan seems to be disturbed in humans, in animals, in all of nature. I ask, "Is God re-adjusting, re-grouping, re-plenishing, re-establishing the laws of nature before our eyes?"

I know prayer can bring about immense change. The

shifting of our thoughts and emotions could and would change our environment, people and events, places and problems. We need to pray. We need to become initiators of change. Man urgently needs to turn fear into hope, hate into peace. Love needs to be magnified in our hearts and minds in order to bring about peace--in order to preserve our earth. The time has arrived for the masses to unite. It's time for mysticism to become commonplace. Didn't Jesus say become like children in order to enter Heaven? Mysticism results in letting go to the child in us, to the unknown, the fantasy, the awe. I feel it's in growing to understand the mysteries and in surrendering to the unknown that this change will come about. Scripture tells us, "People must think of us as Christ's servants, stewards entrusted with the **mysteries** of God."(1 Cor 4:1-2)

For us, now in this generation, it seems to me that the visits from Mother Mary are this teaching, a calling, a gift, a warning, to let us know times are again about to change.

I found it intriguing to read *True Devotion to Mary*, which was written by St. Louis de Monfort in the 16th century. The author wrote, "It is through Mary that the salvation of the world was begun, and it is through Mary that it must be consummated. In the second coming of Christ, Mary has to be made known and revealed by the Holy Spirit in order that through her, Jesus Christ may be known, loved, and served." "When will souls breathe Mary as their bodies breathe air? When this time comes, wonderful things will happen. The Holy Spirit will come in abundance and fill souls to overflowing with gifts, particularly gifts of wisdom to work miracles of peace. The age of Mary will come."

The numerous apparitions by Mary have begun as St. Louis de Montfort predicted nearly 400 years ago. I believe St. Louis' words are true for now. Mary is appearing here in numerous places to help us, to usher in this new era.

I feel that humanity is in the midst of an intuitive awakening. We need to follow our intuitive self, our true self, our soul, if spirituality is to survive and become the heartbeat of the globe. Each of us holds within us the power to change ourselves and the world. We are all made up of great wisdom and great power. We just have to find it. The connection between inner life and outer life is within us all. Each of us needs to ask "Why am I here?" "What is my purpose?" What can I do for the whole? As each of us grows in spirituality and heals, so does the earth, the universe.

Freedom is when one starts taking responsibility for participating in life, actively involving oneself in choices that affect direction and destiny. Most of us look for instant cure, quick fixes. So did I. For me, the call to self- knowledge was not always easy but it has definitely always been interesting, as I've continued to write about unknown realities, about sacred mysteries that are often denied by our systematic, scientific and ecclesiastical life styles.

I like to think I've joined in His harmony, the harmony of the world. I accept God's plan for my life. I have discovered it is essential to feed my soul the same, as it is essential to feed my body. The nourishment for both is imperative. Prayer and meditation refuel and energize me. I've learned to live with purpose. The answer, the essence of life, is in giving and sharing--all for the glory of God. I'm taught newness everyday. I have Divine assistance. I live and breathe with all that is. I've learned I'm a soul with a body, not a body with a soul. I know there is nothing more pleasurable than being a part of this power of God. I pray everyone will feel this force, this energy of life, this power, and that they will learn put it to use. Finding ourselves as co-creators with Christ is helping the world become one with Him. I pray we all learn to know the meaning of the words: "Be still and know that I Am God," and share in His power.

December 3, 1995. It's hard to believe another year has gone by and it's Advent. When Psalm 122 was read, "Come walk in the Light." + I instantly knew the meaning of my vision of November 24th. God was inviting me to walk with Him. I shared my feelings with Fr. Mike at the sign of peace. He nodded and said, "That fits perfectly." I remembered vividly my last Advent and wondered what God had in store for me this year.

On December 5, 1995. I was thrilled to see on the front page of our local newspaper the heading of an article *Spiritual Healing, Re-searcher bridges gap between prayer and science.* I thought, "How appropriate, God, for you to send an affirmation so promptly on my newly completed writings." I read the article with much enthusiasm. Herbert Benson, a Harvard Medical School professor was quoted as saying, "he found the mind could work like a drug, especially among people who have strong faith."

I thanked God, over and over for the affirmation.

December 14, 1995. I had a vision. + As I witnessed much Light, and the eye, I saw thrones of angels. Silhouettes of angels of Light were everywhere. I could see their wings in constant motion. I could see their halos and feel their presence. I saw clearly a silhouette of Mary holding baby Jesus. I reveled in the moment.

Then the entire day was filled with pleasure. I rejoiced when I attended Mass and realized it was the feast of St. John of the Cross, one of my favorite mystics. I thought, "What an appropriate day to be visited by angels."

That night I had a profound dream. + In my dream I was in a large room with a crowd of people who were milling around. I found myself attracted to a man on the side of the room. Few people were around him. As I approached he reached out his hand and touched me. An electrical current went through my body. I looked into His eyes and said, "It's you, Jesus, isn't it? Does anyone else know it's you? Know that you're here?" I asked Him to share more of His power and Light with me. As He placed His arm on my shoulder I collapsed to the floor from the force of the power.

When I awakened I recalled the dream vividly. It had seemed very real. I began to remember the electrical jolts in my visions, the electrical jolts I've felt in being healed, and the electrical jolts in being a vessel of God in using my hands in healings. I gave thanks for the dream of His Ultimate power.

December 22, 1995. I met with Fr. Mike. We discussed the beautiful message our group had recently received concerning hearing God's voice. I commented, "For a long time I've known my + were simply hearing His voice in my heart. I wish all the members in my prayer group recognized this gift." He responded, "Don't worry. I think they will in time."

I then shared with Mike the finding of my relic. Thirty-two years ago, my brother who was studying in Rome brought me back a relic. I put it away in a drawer. I've moved the container around over the years. Last week I happened to think of the relic and wondered who the relic was. I had forgotten. I found the container holding the relic in a drawer beside my bed. When I opened the container I was stunned. I felt power emerge from it. Since I am now so sensitive to energy I placed my hand over the relic and felt energy and warmth radiating from it. I read the inscription and discovered it was St. Jude Thaddeus the Apostle. A feeling of awe came over me. I wondered, "Could this be an original relic from one of the apostles? Could I have had this all these years without paying attention to what I had in my possession?" I found the papers that verified it was a first class relic.

I encouraged Fr. Mike to feel the warmth radiating from the small bone fragment that is encased in a jeweled setting. Mike commented, "Goodness. That is really something, I can sense the warmth. Relics this old are not available today. You're very lucky." He promptly went to his bookshelf and looked for information on St Jude. Mike read, "Jesus and Jude's resemblance were very striking. Some individuals feel St. Jude was the brother of Jesus. St. Jude is the patron of the impossible..." + I immediately interrupted, "Isn't this ironic. My brother who I think doesn't totally understand what all I am experiencing was possibly the one who started this whole overwhelming process by giving me a relic from the saint who

197

is known for the impossible. Amazing! Certainly everything
going on in my life today seems impossible, but is wonderful."
    After we finished reading about St. Jude, I shared with
Mike that Erv and I would be leaving for a month after
Christmas for a winter vacation. I also explained how I had
been receiving mail in an unusual way about a place called
Caritas in Birmingham and that I was thinking about stopping
there. I explained how over the past several weeks, five
envelopes had arrived at my home, which had been previously
opened and resealed with tape. All five were hand addressed
by different handwriting and had different postmarks - Atlanta,
Texas, Birmingham, etc. All were about Caritas explaining
their mission. I wondered if the occurrence was a +? It
seemed so unusual. Were angels gathering the mail and
sending it off to me? I said, "These letters have piqued my
curiosity. We plan to stop there on our way South. All I know
about Caritas is that it is a place where Mother Mary appeared
to Marija, one of the visionaries from Medjugorje, when she
was here in the states donating a kidney to her ailing brother."
    "When will you be there?" Mike asked. I explained that
we were going to my see my mom in Kentucky for a few days
and we would stop at Caritas on January 1. He said, "How
appropriate, that's the feast of the Mother of God." + Chills
abounded. I hadn't thought of that. "I can't believe this," I
said, "Just as I think I'm finishing my writings on Mary more is
already beginning to appear on the horizon. I can feel it in my
heart. God really keeps me busy. I love it." Mike responded,
"Have a wonderful time and I'll be anxious to hear all when
you get back."

    I pray, "Dear Jesus, many thoughts are in my mind. I
thank you for all my blessings this past year. With You
leading the way the year that has flown by so quickly. Thanks
so much for my ongoing new knowledge, my abundant
healings, for the constant joy in my heart. I thank you for all
my visions, God Messages, and inspirations for writing. I
thank you for the powerful messages to our prayer group. I

wonder where you will be leading me in 1996. I know before you came on earth the prophets of old spoke of your coming and of the glorious happenings that would abound. I know you are instructing me as you did those prophets. I know I am writing for you. I know my writings will help others to grow and learn as you have taught me. I wonder how many individuals listen to you? I wonder how many really listened to you when you were present on earth? How many really believed you were Christ? How many have made fun of you? How many didn't believe in the power of healings when they occurred right before their eyes? I wonder how many didn't believe in the power of miracles? I wonder how many believe now in your word, your miracles, and your power? Thank you for the gift of faith, the gift of believing in you. The gift of your Power. The gift of your Love. I know that just as there are doubters and disbelievers in the apparitions of Mary, angels, and miracles, there are also doubters in your presence among us. But I believe and know, that you, your Power, your Spirit are here. You have remained here with us, within us all, and you are just waiting to be acknowledged and realized. You expect us all to continue to help build Your Kingdom. You need us all to help bring about the era of peace. Be with me. Lead me. I'm yours."

I felt angels surround me and heard "Tell the world to pray the following prayer." +

***

Dear Loving God, please be among us, lead us and guide us. Unite us as one in the Power of Your Spirit. Unite the young and the old. Unite the poor and the rich. Unite the weak and the strong. Unite the races and cultures. Mend and heal our broken hearts. Help us to be stewards of your creation. To be servants who bring justice and peace to the world. To be one in love with all, through Jesus the Christ. For this we pray.

Heavenly Text

About the Author

I write for God. He is the "Presence" in my life. I began to write at the request of my daughter who, when she was dying of leukemia, insisted I was to write a book. I agreed I would try some day, but little did I know it was going to be an on-going event. I started out slowly and there has been a building of experiences. In time I started receiving hundreds of unsolicited visions and messages from heaven that guide my writings. I have kept everything in chronological order that has been relayed to me over many years (1985-2010) – thus three volumes.

Humankind is evolving into a higher consciousness. We have forgotten as a whole that we are all "one" and are here on earth to evolve spiritually. We are living in unprecedented times when all of creation is trying to come into balance - a balance in our bodies, a balance with the earth, and a balance with the heavens.

I had to learn that the chaos of this world and my life were but a gift to enable me to grow. It hasn't always been easy, but it has been a wonderful journey. I learned to pay attention to the synchronicity occurrences and intuitive insights in my life. I now receive messages in prayer, meditation, prophetic dreams, visions and experiences throughout the day when encountering a profoundness that demands to be recognized. In time I learned to become an open vessel for the power of God to manifest through me. Laying-on-of-hands and other healing modalities became a part of my life. Knowing and believing in God's power is the key to eternal life.

Made in the USA
Charleston, SC
19 May 2011